AF600654

THE COLLEGIATE MORAL PERSON AS PARTY LITIGANT

A HISTORICAL SYNOPSIS AND COMMENTARY

THE CATHOLIC UNIVERSITY OF AMERICA
CANON LAW STUDIES
No. 251

The Collegiate Moral Person as Party Litigant

A Historical Synopsis and Commentary

BY THE
REV. THOMAS J. KILCULLEN, LL.M., J.C.L.
PRIEST OF THE DIOCESE OF SCRANTON

A DISSERTATION

SUBMITTED TO THE FACULTY OF THE SCHOOL OF CANON LAW OF THE CATHOLIC UNIVERSITY OF AMERICA IN PARTIAL FULFILLMENT OF THE REQUIREMENTS FOR THE DEGREE OF DOCTOR OF CANON LAW

THE CATHOLIC UNIVERSITY OF AMERICA PRESS
WASHINGTON, D. C.
1947

NIHIL OBSTAT:

Joannes Rogg Schmidt, A.B., J.C.D.,

Censor Deputatus.

Washingtonii, die 27 maii, 1947.

IMPRIMATUR:

✠Gulielmus J. Hafey, D.D.

Episcopus Scrantonensis.

Scrantonensis, die 23 iunii, 1947.

Murray & Heister
Washington, D. C.

Printed by
Times and News Publishing Co
Gettysburg, Pa., U. S. A

TO THE BLESSED MOTHER

TABLE OF CONTENTS

PAGE

FOREWORD ix

CHAPTER

I. PRELIMINARY NOTIONS 1
Art. 1. The Collegiate Moral Person in Canon Law 1
A. Definition and Doctrine 1
B. Division and Constitution 5
C. Rights and Cessation 7
Art. 2. The Notion of Procedural Representation 9
Art. 3. The Juridic Position of the English Common Law 13

II. THE COLLEGIATE MORAL PERSON IN ROMAN LAW 16
Art. 1. Legal Foundation and Recognition 16
Art. 2. The Procedural Capacity of the Collegiate Person 19
Art. 3. Procedural Representation for Corporate Persons 21
Art. 4. Legal Remedies Applicable to Collegiate Bodies 24

III. THE COLLEGIATE MORAL PERSON IN TRIALS FROM THE DECRETALS OF GREGORY IX TO THE PRESENT CODE 27
Art. 1. Procedural Capacity 28
A. The Person Itself 28
B. Representative Procedural Rights of Abbots, Prelates and Inferiors 30
C. The Rights of the Community or the Chapter 34
Art. 2. The Criminal Proceedings 36
Art. 3. The Representative for Trials 41
A. Nature of the Office 41
B. The Appointment 43
C. The Rights and the Duties of the Representative 44

TABLE OF CONTENTS (Continued)

CHAPTER PAGE

IV. THE EARLY HISTORY OF THE PROCEDURAL RIGHTS OF ECCLESIASTICAL CORPORATIONS IN ENGLISH COMMON LAW 47
Art. 1. Interrelation of the Common Law with the Canon Law 47
Art. 2. The Medieval (1066-1485) Common Law 50

CANONICAL COMMENTARY

V. CONTENTIOUS ACTIONS BY AND AGAINST THE COLLEGIATE MORAL PERSON 53
Art. 1. Contentious Actions in General 53
Art. 2. Juridic Capacity 59
Art. 3. Jurisdiction Concerning Juristic Persons 62
A. The Privilege of the Forum 63
1. Pre-Code Law 64
2. Code Legislation 66
B. Reserved Competence 72
C. The Necessary Forum 78
D. The Ordinary Forum 90
E. The Competent Forum for Specific Religious Corporations 95

VI. THE CORPORATE REPRESENTATION IN THE CONTENTIOUS TRIAL 98
Art. 1. Procedural Capacity 98
Art. 2. The Judicial Advocates and Procurators for Corporations 108
Art. 3. The Trial in which Corporations are Parties 110

VII. THE CORPORATION IN THE CRIMINAL TRIAL 112
Art. 1. Vicarious Imputation of Corporate Guilt 112
Art. 2. The Canonical Penalties for Corporate Delicts 114
Art. 3. The Criminal Procedural Action Against the Corporation 117

CONCLUSIONS 119

BIBLIOGRAPHY 122

TABLE OF AMERICAN CASES CITED 132

BIOGRAPHICAL NOTE 134

INDEX 135

CANON LAW STUDIES 139

FOREWORD

The corporation is the main topic of this dissertation. It is not without great fear that one should approach the study of this complex concept. One would, to appreciate fully the subject, have to be another Gierke (1841-1921), who spent years in his study of canonical and civil law sources in order to bring the truth of the past to the then modern nineteenth century jurisprudence of Germany, or, perhaps, another great pope and lawyer, such as Innocent IV (1243-1254), to be able to clothe concrete projects in the abstract garb. This might well be the dreamy hope of us all.

In the following study the writer attempts to outline rules of law that pertain to the modern corporate bodies, possessed of untold wealth, composed of thousands of stockholders, standing side by side with the ecclesiastical corporate body—poor in spirit—yet both governed by the same basic rules. The former may be conceived of as mother or parent of other corporate groups, lending themselves to further civic, social and economic development; the latter, as likewise capable of parenthood, but limited in its aims or objects to those defined ends which are spiritual in nature.

Except where a treatment is required, the writer will not concern himself with the corporate personality *in se*. Other writers have amply discussed this matter, and reference to their works will be noted in the text for the aid of the reader. Of necessity, then, the present work will be limited to one of the rights of the corporation, that is, its right to bring suit and in suit to offer a defense, in both contentious and criminal cases. Of course, since the ecclesiastical corporate person has civil as well as ecclesiastical rights, these rights will be analyzed from the viewpoint of both spheres of action. Criminal responsibility will be treated, but civil responsibility for tortious acts of the corporation will not be overlooked.

The modern corporation, be it authorized by Church or by State law, must trace its history back to the dim past of early history, where faint traces of the idea of artificial personality may be seen. The great Roman jurisprudence grasped the thought and developed it. Classical antiquity in decisive strokes necessarily shaped the thought. Medieval publicists, the schoolmen, great popes and lawyers were instrumental in designing the further development of the factual entity.

The modern states in both hemispheres have incorporated the moral person. Some have accepted the Roman theory in full, as it was developed by the canonists of the Church; others have retained one phase or another of the Roman thought, mixed with the varied thought of other sources of developed jurisprudence.

Catholics may well be proud that in this field as in others the Church, in producing great thinkers, has aided—as might be expected from a divinely instituted society—in the determination of the basic truths of corporate law. It is a truism that whenever man has strayed in this point from the Church's guidance he has also begun, as a dire effect of his banal pride and arrogance, to create what might be properly called "Frankensteins Incorporated."

The citations from the English Year Books are taken from a secondary source, inasmuch as the primary source is not available to the writer.

The writer wishes to acknowledge the personal kindness of the Most Reverend William J. Hafey, Bishop of Scranton, Pennsylvania, for his permission for advanced study at the Catholic University of America. The writer also wishes to take this opportunity to acknowledge most sincerely his gratitude to the President and Council of Mount Saint Mary's College and Seminary, Emmitsburg, Maryland, for the opportunity of graduate study in Canon Law, and for its many kind acts to the writer. A debt of gratitude is hereby acknowledged to the Faculty of the School of Canon Law of the Catholic University of America for assistance in the preparation of this dissertation, and to all others who have in any way made this work possible.

CHAPTER I

Preliminary Notions

Article 1. The Collegiate Moral Person in Canon Law

A. *Definition and Doctrine*

Ecclesiastical Law has recognized in the course of its great progress through the centuries two distinct classes of persons: one, the physical or natural person, the other, the moral or juridical person. The physical person is capable of rights and duties (*subiectum iuris capax*) in the Church of Christ. The fundamental concept in the recognition of physical persons, in all juridical thought, has been the ability of the person to possess rights and duties. This, rather than the individual's rationality and independence of existence, is the notion behind such recognition.

In the Church the initiation through the sacrament of Christian grace—baptism—creates the legal effects of rights and duties for the one baptized.[1] From the moment of baptism the law grants to the recipient of baptism certain rights. Since members of a society can not have rights without corresponding duties, the Church demands of the baptized individual that he conform to the duties imposed on him by law. Rights and duties are necessarily correlative. Every duty must be a duty towards some person or persons in whom a correlative right is vested. The converse also is true, that every right must be a right against some person or persons upon whom devolves a correlative duty. Every right or duty involves, therefore, a bond of legal obligation.

The moral or juridical person exists as a legal entity established by Canon Law. This legal person, unlike the physical or natural person, is the creature of the Church. The Church constitutes it, giving it a licit life by due recognition.[2] This moral being or person

[1] Canon 87.
[2] Canon 99.

is to Canon Law what the modern corporation is to the jurisprudence of other legal systems. The ecclesiastical moral person is known in the Code of Canon Law under various titles. For example, it is known as a *persona iuridica,*[3] *ens iuridicum,*[4] and, finally, as a *persona moralis.*[5] In the Code of Canon Law, which went into effect on May 19, 1918, there is lacking a definition of the juristic person. This omission was a wise precaution on the part of the legislator, because even in the Roman Law definitions in jurisprudence were considered dangerous.[6]

However, for the purpose in hand it seems mandatory to explore the limitations and extensions of the complex concept known as the moral person or the corporation. The moral person may be defined as: that which, besides physical persons, is capable of rights and obligations.[7] Perhaps a clearer expression of the thought is the following: that which, besides physical persons, has the capacity of possessing and exercising rights in the Church according to the sacred canons.[8] Both these definitions imply a being or something which in reality has existence in law

Coronata teaches that the true theory of the nature of the juridic person seems to be that which holds that the moral person is based on the real association of the members.[9] This may properly be called the Realist Theory. Standing opposite this theory is another view of the basic juridic nature of the moral person which is called the Fiction Theory. But the Fiction Theory receives little support

---

[3] Canon 687.

[4] Canon 1409.

[5] Canon 99.

[6] D. (50, 17) 202—"Omnis definitio in iure periculosa est: parum est enim ut non subverti possit."

[7] Coronata, *Institutiones Iuris Canonici* (5 vols., Vol. I-IV editio altera aucta et emendata, Vols. I-II, 1939; Vol. III, 1941; Vol. IV, 1945; Vol. V, 1936, Romae: Marietti), I, n. 135 (hereafter cited as *Institutiones*).

[8] Blat, *Commentarium Textus Codicis Iuris Canonici* (5 vols. in 7, Romae: Ex Typographia Pontificia in Instituto Pii IX, 1921-1938. Lib. I, 1921; Lib. II, editio altera, 1921; Lib. II, partes II, III, ed. tertia, 1938; Lib. III, Pars I, 2. ed. aucta et emendata, 1924; Lib. III, partes II-VI, 2. ed. examinata denuo et aucta, 1934; Lib. IV, 1927; Lib. V, 1924), II, n. 29 (hereafter cited as *Commentarium*).

[9] Coronata, *Institutiones,* I, n. 135.

from the modern canonists.[10] It is to be noted that the capacity for possessing and exercising rights and obligations can not be exercised by the moral being of itself (*per se*), but must be exercised through the entity's representative or representatives. This most noteworthy feat of legal imagination, then, is a legal person or subject to which the law attributes a purely legal personality. There is implied a legal constitution or establishment of persons who are not men.

Since the counterpart of the ecclesiastical moral person is found in Common Law jurisdictions, it seems indicated to search also for a definition of the secular corporation. But first a remark should be inserted about the terms Civil Law and Common Law.

When the term Civil Law is properly used it means the Roman Law.[11] However, the term is often used to mean the law of those jurisdictions which is based, directly or indirectly, on Roman Law.[12] Again, and perhaps improperly, in both the United States and England, the term Civil Law has become a convenient title by which the law of the land is distinguished from other forms of law. Such law is that of the state or *civitas*. The term is also used to distinguish parts of the law of the state and not the whole law of the land. Thus the term is used as opposed to the terms criminal law or military law.[13]

In this dissertation the term Civil Law will refer solely to the Roman Law, with one clear exception, namely, when it is used in non-canonical references in contradistinction to the term criminal law. In Canon Law the term contentious, rather than civil, will be used to distinguish litigation of a non-criminal nature. If reference is made to modern jurisdictions which base their particular law either directly or indirectly on the Roman Law, the term modern Civil Law will be used.

---

[10] Wernz, *Ius Decretalium* (2. ed., 6 vols., Romae et Prati, 1906-1913), VI, 24.

[11] Bouvier, *Law Dictionary* (3. rev. ed., 2 vols., St. Paul, Minn.: West Publishing Company, 1914), I, ad v. "Civil Law."

[12] Webster, *New International Dictionary* (2. ed., Springfield, Mass.: G. & C. Merriam Company, 1942), ad v. "Civil Law."

[13] Salmond, *Jurisprudence* (7. ed., London: Sweet & Maxwell, 1924), p. 35. LeBuffe-Hayes, *Jurisprudence* (3. rev. ed., New York: Fordham University Press, 1938), p. 67.

There remains one other term, namely Common Law, which will warrant a definition. Common Law refers to the jurisprudence of the United States of America, with a few exceptions, and to the law of England. These jurisdictions do not follow Roman Law, although they have been somewhat influenced by it. The term Common Law simply means that law which is not based on Roman Law, arising from principles, usages and rules which do not rest for their authority upon any express and positive declaration of the will of the legislature.[14] The legal enactments of legislatures are classified as statutory law.

The non-ecclesiastical or secular corporation may now be defined as: "A body, consisting of one or more natural persons, established by law, usually for some specific purpose, and continued by a succession of members."[15] In Common Law jurisprudence no two authorities are in accord as to just what the corporation is in its true juridic nature.[16] Some authorities are of the opinion that the concept of a corporation is very close to that of a natural person. The German theory, or, as it is sometimes called, the association theory, which was followed by the eminent English scholar, Sir Frederick Pollock (1845-1937), regards the corporation as acquiring an organic character which qualifies it to participate in the life of the state.

On the other hand, there are some authorities who hold that the corporate person is a fiction. For example, Mr. Justice Oliver Wendell Holmes (1841-1935) wrote to Professor I. Maurice Wormser of Fordham University School of Law on December 19, 1923, that he regarded the conception of corporate personality as a fiction. The Justice added, however: "But as I said when young, on the Massachusetts bench, the very meaning of the fiction is that you are to act as if it were true."[17]

---

[14] Bouvier, *op. cit.*, I, ad v. "Common Law"; Holmes, *The Common Law* (Boston: Little, Brown & Company, 1943), pp. 34-38.

[15] Bouvier, *op. cit.*, I, ad. v. "Corporation."

[16] Cf. Wormser, *Disregard of the Corporate Fiction and Allied Corporation Problems* (New York: Baker, Voorhis and Company, 1929), p. 3; Anderson, *Limitations of the Corporate Entity* (St. Louis, Mo.: Thomas Law Book Co., 1931), § 4.

[17] Wormser, *op. cit.*, p. 6.

In the celebrated case of Dartmouth College v. Woodward[18] the Chief Justice Marshall (1755-1835) defined the corporation as "an artificial being, invisible, intangible, and existing only in contemplation of law." This definition followed Lord Coke's (1552-1634) and Mr. Justice Blackstone's (1723-1780) legal thought on the corporate entity. But, following the German theory, corporations in this country have been convicted for such personal crimes as grand larceny, and the knowing and intentional deposit of obscene matter in the United States mails.[19]

B. *Division and Constitution*

The Catholic Church itself and the Holy See have the character of a moral person by divine institution.[20]

The Church constitutes the inferior moral person, giving it life by due recognition.[21] This legal person, when duly constituted in law, becomes, like the natural person, a *subiectum iuris capax*, or capable of exercising rights and duties.[22] Legal constitution or recognition can be had in either of two ways. The moral person can be constituted by the law itself, or by a special concession of the competent legal superior in the form of a decree.[23] This recognition, whether by law or by decree, is dependent on two alternate primary requisites. The end or purpose of the group must be religious or charitable.[24]

As mentioned, the Holy See and the Catholic Church have the nature of a legal person by direct divine enactment. But inferior moral bodies, sharing in the divine commission, may be constituted by the Church, and hence any civil power is incompetent to create these bodies, since these bodies are dependent on the Church, and must be supported by it in the fulfillment of its ends and in the

---

[18] 4 Wheat. 518, 636.

[19] United States v. New York Herald Co., 159 Fed. 296; United States v. MacAndrews & Forbes Co., 149 Fed. 823.

[20] Canon 100, § 1.

[21] Canon 99.

[22] Regatillo, *Institutiones Iuris Canonici* (2 vols., Santander: Sal Terrae, 1941-1942), I, 118.

[23] Canon 100, § 1.

[24] Canon 100, § 1.

selection of the means to the end. No juristic person can, therefore, exist in the Church if it does not derive its authority from the Church.[25] But, being subordinate to the Church, whose mission is supernatural, these moral persons have an end which is in accord with the general purpose of the Church.

The end of the purely civil corporations, on the other hand, is of necessity different from that of the canonical moral person. The civil corporation has its existence, in Common Law jurisdictions, only by the act of the sovereign authority and not by the Common Law itself.[26]

In order to understand the second requisite for the erection of the ecclesiastical moral bodies, one must note that the moral person has a structural division which is distinguishable into, first, the collegiate or corporate body, and secondly, the non-collegiate or non-corporate.[27] The distinction between the two brings to the foreground the second requisite for the establishment of the non-collegiate and for the constitution of the collegiate body respectively. The distinction lies in this that the collegiate body is composed of physical persons. Such, for example, would be the confraternity or the chapter.[28] The establishment of the collegiate moral person in Canon Law postulates at least three persons or incorporators.[29] The individuals of the group are incorporated to constitute the moral personality.[30] The collegiate moral person, once erected, stands independently of its members.

The non-collegiate moral person, on the other hand, is not supported by physical persons, but it is not to be inferred that this support would not be essential for the *de facto* existence of the person.[31] The non-collegiate person, as an instituted *ens iuridicum,* is totally independent of the collection of persons which may form its *de facto* basis,[32] so that the non-collegiate moral person is in

[25] Cappello, *Summa Iuris Publici Ecclesiastici* (Romae, 1923), n. 40 (hereafter cited as *Summa*).

[26] Anderson, *op. cit.,* §§ 3, 9.

[27] Canon 99.

[28] Regatillo, *op. cit.,* I, 118.

[29] Canon 100, § 2.

[30] Wernz, *Ius Decretalium,* VI, 24.

[31] Coronata, *Institutiones,* I, n. 138.

[32] Coronata, *loc. cit.*

fact and in law an institution or an aggregate of property, real or personal, which has a defined end, and in virtue of which the so-called *fundus* becomes the subject of rights and duties.[33] Hospitals, seminaries, benefices and orphan asylums are considered to be non-collegiate moral persons.

In Common Law jurisdictions, as a general thing, corporations are of two classes, namely, corporations aggregate and corporations sole. The aggregate corporation is an incorporated group of co-existing persons, while the corporation sole is that type which has only one member at a time.[34] However, since the legal person is a creature of the law, there may well be a type in which the *corpus* is an institution, such as a library or a hospital; or, it may be a type in which the *corpus* would be some estate or fund devoted to some specific purpose—a charitable fund, for example. These particular variations of the concept would depend upon the law of the particular territory. For the present purpose it suffices simply to point out the general scheme.[35]

C. *Rights and Cessation*

The ecclesiastical moral person, once duly constituted, has all the rights and obligations which a physical person has, with the exception of those which are excluded from the moral person's sphere either because of its nature or by the intervention of positive law.[36] The manner of exercising these rights and obligations will vary with the nature of the collegiate and the non-collegiate person. The collegiate moral person, unless prohibited, has the right of having binding rules to guide it in such corporate internal and external management as would concern the manner of electing officers; the administration of its goods and affairs; and any other sphere of operation which would come under the end for which it exists.[37] These rights and obligations remain with the moral person even

---

[33] Vermeersch-Creusen, *Epitome Iuris Canonici* (4. ed., 3 vols., Mechliniae-Romae :H. Dessain, 1929-1931), I, 146 (hereafter cited *Epitome*).

[34] Salmond, *Jurisprudence*, p. 339.

[35] Salmond, *op. cit.*, pp. 337-338.

[36] Coronata, *op. cit.*, I, n. 139.

[37] Coronata, *loc. cit.*

though only one member, after incorporation, exists in the body. But these rights of the corporate body are protected in a special way, for the legal person is regarded in law as a minor.[38]

The Common Law corporation is in like manner recognized as having rights and obligations similar to those of the ecclesiastical legal person, and is protected, perhaps, to the same extent in these rights. It has the right to formulate binding by-laws; the right to sue and the capacity of being sued, and continues to exist even though only one member, after incorporation, exists in the body.[39]

The corporation, whether of ecclesiastical or of civil or common law origin, possesses in its very nature the element of perpetuity. In Canon Law the corporate person does not become extinct until it is either suppressed by legitimate authority or has ceased to reveal any outward marks of existence for a period of one hundred years.[40]

In Common Law the corporation is capable of indefinite duration, but not incapable of extinction or dissolution. As a general rule, the corporation does not lose its life with the disappearance of its *corpus*. It may be dormant, but it is not dead. Whether particular statutes in the various Common Law jurisdictions actually prescribe limitations for a period of dormant corporate life is not of any concern for the present. The general rule as aforementioned may of course have to be amended in those jurisdictions where the fiction theory is not adopted.[41]

These legal beings, like natural persons, are protected by the Canon Law in acts which, when performed through external force or compulsion, could not be resisted. Acts thus performed are considered invalid acts.[42]

Since the being under consideration is a *subiectum iuris capax*, it necessarily follows that it must have the remedial right of going into court to have its substantive rights protected or vindicated. It is now necessary to give a brief outline of the procedural remedy which avails in behalf of these persons.[43]

---

[38] Canon 100, § 3.

[39] Bouvier, *op. cit.*, ad v. "Corporation."

[40] Canon 102, § 1.

[41] Cf. Salmond, *op. cit.*, p. 351.

[42] Canon 103, § 1.

[43] Canon 1552, § 1.

ARTICLE 2. THE NOTION OF PROCEDURAL REPRESENTATION

There is no part of Canon Law which is so wholly based on Roman Law as that of the law of procedure. Roman law was based on the natural principles of equity and justice; it influenced the law of the Church from the time of the Christian emperors.

Representation at trials for individual litigants is frequently mentioned in the canonical literature of the Middle Ages. And, with the development of the legal personality of the collegiate moral body and the concomitant need for procedural representation for these bodies, it will be seen that in the sources there developed a particular type of representative for them in judicial procedure. The representative for the corporate bodies was designated by various names, but particularly by the title *syndicus*. In the Decretals of Gregory IX (1227-1241) there is to be found a heading *de syndico,* immediately following the heading or title *de procuratoribus.* As a matter of fact, it was not until the present Code of Canon Law was enacted that legislative parlance relinquished the particular designation of syndic for the representative of a corporate person.

The reason for this departure from the pre-Code legislative terminology for this particular type of procedural representative was probably the fact, as will be set forth later in Chapters II and III, that in the final analysis the syndic was a species of procurator. These two individuals in their capacity of representatives were distinguishable only in this that the procurator represented the physical person while the syndic represented the juridical being. Be that as it may, in the sources there appears a distinctive type of representative at judicial proceedings in behalf of the moral person. In the present historical synopsis it is to that type of representative that special consideration is to be given. However, in offering these preliminary notions of the subject, the writer deemed advisable to touch briefly by way of preparation on modern law as governing the representative at trials, in order that the juridical position of the historical representative might be better understood in its true light.

Canon Law today uses the term process in a generic sense to designate the method of adjusting the rights of its subjects even in an extra-judicial manner, while it employs the specific term judgment to signify the strictly judicial procedure.[44] The term *iudicium ecclesiasticum* points to a legal discussion and settlement, before a duly constituted court, of a disputed matter over which the Church is judicially competent.[45]

In every contentious case there is a plaintiff and a defendant. The plaintiff makes a charge, and the defendant seeks to answer it. Any person, as a general rule, may sue, or in other words be a plaintiff, unless the Code prohibits him from doing so.[46] The terms which the Code uses in designation of a plaintiff and a defendant are *actor* and *reus*. All defendants must appear in court when they are duly and legally summoned, and then offer their reply to the charge that is brought against them.[47]

If the trial is concerned with the declaration of juridical facts, or with the prosecution or vindication of a person's rights, whether it be in behalf of a physical person or a moral one, then the trial is known as a contentious one. Trials concerned with the infliction or with the declaration of a penalty are known as criminal trials.[48]

The collegiate moral person is represented in court by the one who is its rector or administrator, except in special cases. If there is a conflict between the rights of the legal person and those of its administrator or rector, the ordinary must be petitioned for the appointment of a procurator to represent the legal person in the trial.[49] Prelates and superiors of chapters, of sodalities and of any other *collegium*, must first obtain the consent of the corporate body in the manner defined by its statutes before they appear in court in the potential capacity of representatives.[50]

The local ordinary himself may either personally or through a delegate appear in court for the legal persons who are under his jurisdiction, whenever the administrators of such persons fail to prosecute or defend the interests involved, or show neglect in

[44] Cf. Noval, *Commentarium Codicis Iuris Canonici*, Liber IV, *De Processibus*, Pars I, *De Iudiciis* (Romae: Augustae Taurinorum, 1920), p. 1 (hereafter cited as *De Iudiciis*).

[45] Canon 1552, § 1.

[46] Canon 1646.

[47] Canon 1646.

[48] Canon 1552, § 2, 1°, 2°.

[49] Canon 1649.

[50] Canon 1653, § 3.

prosecuting or defending the rights which are at stake.[51] Only that superior of a religious organization may appear as a plaintiff or as a defendant who is authorized by its constitutions to do so.[52]

When a representative is appointed to stand in trial for the collegiate moral person (*procurator ad litem*), this representative must comply with certain rules. The judge will not permit the procurator to plead in the case until he has deposited in court a special written mandate of the party whom he represents in the litigation. The procedural representative is elected by the collegiate moral person according to the manner prescribed for corporate action in canon 101. Or the representative may be delegated by anyone so empowered to designate or select him for his authorized capacity in the trial.

In both cases a mandate must be given to the person so designated if he is to act as representative. This mandate in its specific import must appear at the foot of the summons, duly signed by the party represented, together with an indication of the place and date. Indication must be made in writing that the person issuing the mandate does not know how to write, if that is the fact, and a pastor, or a notary of the curia, or two witnesses, shall sign the mandate in his or her stead.[53] The mandate which authorized the procurator must be preserved along with the other acts of the case.[54]

The representative is by law limited in the scope of his capacity when but a simple mandate has been issued to him. In order to renounce any of the judicial acts, or the suit itself, or the instance in which it is being heard or in future can be prosecuted, or even to make a friendly settlement of the case, he would need a special mandate. Likewise, he could not take an oath, or ask the other party to take an oath, nor could he arbitrate the disputed matter apart from a specific mandate authorizing such specific intervention.[55]

---

[51] Canon 1653, § 5.
[52] Canon 1653, § 6.
[53] Canon 1659.
[54] Canon 1660.
[55] Canon 1662.

A procurator *ad litem,* although duly appointed by his principal, may be rejected by the court for a just cause.[56] A just cause would obtain if the procurator were a non-Catholic, or also a religious as long as the latter is not representing his own organization.[57] Again, one of the parties may petition the court for the removal of the procurator *ad litem.*[58] Finally, the party who constituted the procurator may likewise remove him. The removal does not take effect until notice thereof has been given to the procurator. If the joining of issues (*contestatio litis*) has taken place, the removal to become effective must be accompanied with a notice to the judge and the other party. After the final sentence has been rendered, the procurator has the right and the duty to make the appeal, if the principal does not object.[59]

The representative must act in accordance with law and with the best interests of his principal in view. All illegal agreements involving maintenance and champerty, or if made in consideration of an exorbitant recompense, will be held invalid. Moreover, the representative will be subject to certain punishments for such conduct, as also for his failure to handle his principal's affairs in court in good faith.[60]

The bill of complaint may be signed by the procurator.[61] The summons must be presented to that person who in the name of the principal must answer in the trial.[62] If the procurator has been the cause of the discharge of the suit through a discontinuance of its prosecution, the moral person may sue for damages.[63] The judge may *ex officio* introduce witnesses in cases in which a corporation is the party, since in law such a corporation is deemed equivalent in status to minors.[64]

---

[56] Canon 1663.
[57] Canon 1657.
[58] Canon 1663.
[59] Canon 1664.
[60] Canons 1665; 1666.
[61] Canon 1708.
[62] Canon 1713.
[63] Canon 1737.
[64] Canon 1759, § 3.

ARTICLE 3. THE JURIDIC POSITION OF THE ENGLISH COMMON LAW

In Chapter IV of this dissertation a study will be made of the English Common Law in regard to the canonical corporation. In that Chapter a conspectus of this field of law will be made from secondary sources, to discover first what developments in English Common Law may be attributable to an ecclesiastical source in regard to corporations, and, secondly, to what extent the canonical corporation was recognized in early English law.

In the present article the reasons for considering the corporate principles of the English Common Law, in so far as they pertain to the topic under discussion, will be set forth. This will necessitate a brief preliminary outline of the basic juridic nature of both Church and State, as well as of the sovereign and absolute right of both Church and State to create and recognize inferior moral bodies within their respective spheres of action.

By the term English Common Law is meant that system of law which has prevailed in England in contradistinction to the other great systems, such as the Roman or civil law.[65] As stated in Article 1, the term Common Law is used in its strict sense to designate those principles, rules and usages which govern actions applicable to persons and property, but which do not rest on any positive will of the legislature.

The Catholic Church and the Apostolic See have the nature of a legal person by divine ordinance.[66] The Catholic Church claims a divine foundation, inasmuch as its founder, Christ, came into the world to establish the Church as the Kingdom of God. This Kingdom was composed of a plurality of persons, and their corporate rights were embodied in a visible head of this society. The constitution of the Church determines the nature of its mission,[67] which is the same as that for which Christ came into the world.

This end is plainly supernatural or spiritual, but it does not mean

---

[65] Bouvier, *Law Dictionary,* I, ad. v. "Common Law."

[66] Canon 100, § 1.

[67] Leo XIII, ep. encycl., *Satis cognitum,* 29 iun. 1896—*Codicis Iuris Canonici Fontes,* cura Emī Petri Card. Gasparri editi (9 vols., Romae [postea Civitate Vaticana]: Typis Polyglottis, 1923-1939; Vols. VII-IX ed. cura et studio Emī Iustiniani Card. Serédi), n. 630 (hereafter cited *Fontes*).

to exclude the use of temporal means to achieve the primary end. Authority, for the direction of the society to the end for which it was founded, was reposed in St. Peter.[68] This was a supreme and as such an indivisible power. The stability of this Kingdom of God on earth has the element of perpetuity and continuity which one finds in other corporate bodies. The authority, to be exercised properly, requires a legislative,[69] a coercive[70] and a judiciary power.[71] This, too, is inherent in the Church.

There are many canons in the Code which safeguard the Church's independence, and vindicate her rights and freedom of action as a moral person and as a perfect society.[72] Now, a moral person[73] endowed with such rights is termed a perfect society, that is, a society which enjoys not only full independence in its existence, but complete control of all the necessary and useful means proportionate to the end for which the society exists.[74] There are but two species of societies juridically perfect in their own order: the Church and the State.[75] By the term *Church* is to be understood the One Universal Church.

The State is a necessary juridical society in view precisely of the social character, condition and nature of man. There is present in both societies—in the Church and in the State—a juridic bond which unites men in either of these groups for the attainment of their respective ends.[76] Each of these societies is supreme in its own order and completely autonomous within its indicated sphere. But both the supremacy and the independence of the juridically

---

[68] St. Matth., XVI; 19-20.

[69] Cappello, *Summa,* n. 70.

[70] Tarquini, *Institutiones Iuris Publici Ecclesiastici* (4. ed., Romae, 1865), n. 20.

[71] Cappello, *op. cit.,* n. 77; Tarquini, *op. cit.,* n. 21.

[72] Canons, 100, § 1; 218-219; 1352; 1375; 1384; 1495; 1499; 1518; 1552-1559; 2214.

[73] Canon 100, § 1, vindicates the status of moral personality for the Catholic Church *"ex ipsa ordinatione divina."*

[74] Ottaviani, *Institutiones Iuris Publici Ecclesiastici* (2. ed., 2 vols., Civitate Vaticana: Typis Polyglottis, 1935-1936), I, n. 26.

[75] Leo XIII, ep. encycl. *Immortale Dei,* 1 nov. 1885—*Fontes,* n. 592.

[76] Cappello, *Institutiones Iuris Publici Ecclesiastici* (2 vols., Romae: Taurinorum Augustae, 1907-1908), I, 17.

perfect society must be understood in a relative sense, that is, each *in its kind* is supreme, each has *fixed* limits or spheres of action.[77]

Since man has a twofold destiny, he must seek his natural end in the social order, and his supernatural end in the order of grace, to which order he has been elevated by a very special intervention on the part of God. Man's care then has been divided between the State and the Church.[78] In consequence of this, both societies may constitute or erect the legal moral person to serve the needs of man, the one society doing so in the temporal order, the other, in the spiritual order.

However, it is to be noted that modern canonists maintain that the creative act of the State is not absolutely necessary for the establishment of the civil juristic person, i.e., the corporation. These canonists maintain that it is the natural right of man to form these bodies for the achievement of purely natural ends. And since natural rights are not the result of legislation by the State, but rather precede all positive civil laws, man's development in society is not exclusively produced by the State.[79] While the Church will recognize a duly constituted corporation of a State, the State does not, in every instance, similarly recognize the corporate body duly constituted by the Church. In the United States all corporations must be constituted or created by the authority of the State. The American Law does not recognize the right of the Church to establish a juridical person.

---

[77] Tarquini, *op. cit.*, n. 55.

[78] Leo XIII, ep. encycl. *Immortale Dei*, 1 nov. 1885—*Fontes*, n. 592.

[79] Cappello, *Summa*, n. 50; Ottaviana, *op. cit.*, I, n. 27.

CHAPTER II

The Collegiate Moral Person in Roman Law

ARTICLE 1. LEGAL FOUNDATION AND RECOGNITION

The term Civil Law, as used in this dissertation, is the law of the Roman Empire (*Corpus Iuris Civilis*) as opposed to Canon Law (*Corpus Iuris Canonici*). The term Roman Law, in its most extensive meaning, includes all those legal principles and rules which were in force among the Romans, regardless of the time they were enacted or adopted. In a more restrictive sense, however, the term connotes the law compiled under the Emperor Justinian.[1] The term Canon Law, on the other hand, denotes the body of ecclesiastical law of the Roman Catholic Church relating to matters over which the Church has jurisdiction.

Roman Law as understood in the restrictive sense was still in force, in some degree at least, in the modern states of Europe until recent times. In America, Roman Law is indirectly the foundation of the law in Canada, Mexico, Louisiana, and all the Republics of South America. There is a diversity of opinion regarding its influence on the Common Law of England.

The evolution and development of the concept of the juristic person began with the advanced jurisprudence of the Romans.[2] The ancient Romans had only a vague concept or notion of the legal personality in law which enjoyed rights and was responsible for its actions. There were ancient religious *sodalitates* and certain *collegia* which, during the Republic, could be formed with little or no restriction. They had various objects or aims, such as those of

---

[1] Bouvier, *op. cit.*, I, ad. v. "Civil Law."

[2] Brown, *The Canonical Juristic Personality with Special Reference to its Status in the United States of America,* The Catholic University of America Canon Law Studies, n. 39, Washington, D. C.: The Catholic University of America, 1927), p. 8 (hereafter cited *Juristic Personality*).

friendly societies, burial clubs and trade organizations. But whether they had corporate character remains obscure.[3]

It is certain that merely being a lawful *collegium* did not necessarily imply a corporate character. It was not until 7 B. C. that all newly formed *collegia* required, for their existence, authorization or permission from the civil society. It cannot be concluded even from the mere fact of authorization as accorded by the state that these bodies were corporations in the now accepted meaning of the word, unless of course there was a special grant of juristic personality in the individual case. And this was so until the late Classical Period.[4]

At the close of the Republic, municipalities were brought under the domain of private law. After this period they held property not as *res publicae* but as private owners. At least to this extent municipalities had the legal status of private individuals.[5]

It was not until the advent of the Empire that the concept of the corporate person was introduced into Roman private law.[6] In the Empire no *collegia* could be established without the intervention of legal authority, and those which earlier were in existence required an act of confirmation for any continued legal existence.[7] After the examples of the municipalities, lawful societies such as the *collegium,* the *sodalitas* and the *universitas,* were then recognized as having proprietary capacity in private law.

The Romans gave full protection to the rights of the corporations.[8] This was especially true in reference to bequests or legacies to monasteries, churches and certain charitable corporate bodies.[9]

[3] William Smith, *Dictionary of Greek and Roman Antiquities* (2 vols., London, 1890), I, 470, ad v. "collegium."

[4] Buckland, *A Manual of Roman Private Law* (2. ed., Cambridge: University Press, 1939), pp. 35-46.

[5] Sohm, *The Institutes of Roman Law,* translated by Ledlie (3. ed., Oxford, 1926), p. 102 (hereafter referred to as *Institutes*).

[6] Sohm-Ledlie, *op. cit.,* p. 189.

[7] D. (3, 4) (1, 1).

[8] C. (1, 2) 22.

[9] C. (1, 2) 22: "Sancimus res ad venerabiles ecclesias vel xenones vel monasteria vel ptochotrophia vel brephotrophia vel orphanotrophia vel gerontocomia vel si quid tale consortium descendentes ex qualicumque curiali liberalitate sive inter vivos sive mortis causa sive in ultimis voluntatibus habita lucrativorum inscriptionibus liberas immunesque esse."

While the legal sources offer numerous instances of authoritative recognition of moral or corporate bodies, there is wanting in the Roman Law itself, and also in the writings of the Roman jurists, any definition of a moral person.[10] Further, the admission has to be made that there exist no texts which call the *universitas* a *persona,* and also none which designate it even as a *persona ficta.*[11]

There were two kinds of moral persons in the Roman law; the *universitas personarum,* or the collegiate moral person,[12] and the *universitas bonorum,* or the institute or foundation.[13] The distinction between the two was that the collegiate moral person, i.e., the *universitas personarum,* was a group of persons combined for some definite legal object, end or purpose, e.g., that of mining, of fishing, or of promoting some charitable cause, as was done for example by a burial club. The institute or foundation—the *universitas bonorum*—on the other hand, was not so much concerned with the associating of persons, but rather with the collecting of goods, as was done for example through a foundation or an institute of a pious nature.[14]

Ecclesiastical organizations were recognized as moral persons under Justinian Law. No mention, indeed, was made of the corporate body in the *Institutes* of Justinian, but the *Digest* and the *Code* furnish the legal sources on the matter.[15] These constituted the mold or the model from which the later Church Law fashioned the ecclesiastical juristic person with the same structural division as that of the Roman Law.

---

[10] Brown, *Juristic Personality,* p. 17.

[11] Gierke, *Political Theories of the Middle Ages,* translated, with an introduction, by Maitland (Cambridge: University Press, 1922), from the Introduction, p. xviii.

[12] Wernz-Vidal, *Ius Canonicum* (7 vols. in 9, Romae: Universitas Gregoriana, 1927-1946. Vol. I, 1938; Vol. II, 3. ed., a P. Philippo Aguirre recognita, 1943; Vol. III, 1933; Vol. IV, Pars I, 1934; Vol. IV, Pars II, 1935; Vol. V, 3. ed., a P. Philippo Aguirre recognita, 1946; Vol. VI, 1927; Vol. VI, Pars altera, 1928; Vol. VII, 1937), II, n. 25 (hereafter cited *Ius Canonicum*).

[13] Wernz-Vidal, *Ius Canonicum,* II, n. 26.

[14] Sohm-Ledlie, *Institutes,* p. 195.

[15] Sherman, *Roman Law in the Modern World* (2. ed., 3 vols., New York: Baker Voorhis & Co., 1927), III, 994.

The Church, under the Roman Law, was considered a moral person of a distinctive type. It differed from other Roman corporations in that it did not require the civil (Roman) approbation or seal of approval, since the State recognized the sovereignty of the Church. However, it is rather difficult to speak of any legal recognition of this sort during the first three centuries of the Empire.

But certainly through Constantine (306-337) a period of religious liberty was ushered in with a consequent recognition of the Church as a perfect and sovereign society. The Church was deemed a perfect society, capable of exercising corporate rights, and capable of creating certain other inferior moral bodies, through which it might achieve its end or purpose. And the Church was also recognized as capable of exercising rights of a temporal kind or nature. This recognition continued—for it was due to the Church as a divine institution—but with some evolutionary changes of varying degrees.[16]

The private corporation (*universitas personarum*) in order to be recognized legally, required three physical or natural incorporators.[17] But, after incorporation, it could continue to exist as long as there remained even a single member in the moral body.[18] And so the corporation was of its very nature a being endowed with perpetuity.[19] Since this juristic creation of the state was in and of itself incapable of acting in behalf of its own interests, the corporation required some physical person to direct its external actions. This was accomplished through the *magister universitatis*.[20] Under the general principles of the law of representation, the *magister universitatis* acted for and on behalf of the corporation as a guardian did for his minor. He had authority of a derivative nature.

ARTICLE 2. THE PROCEDURAL CAPACITY OF THE COLLEGIATE PERSON

It is needless to stress the point that the Roman Law of private procedure developed as did any other field of the law. Perhaps in

[16] Brown, *Juristic Personality*, pp. 27-28.
[17] D. (50, 16) 85.
[18] D. (3, 4) (7, 2).
[19] D. (3, 4) (7, 2).
[20] D. (46, 8) 9.

line with the changing cultural conditions of the Romans at particular times, a change in the positive rules of procedure is noticeable in the field of the organization of the courts and in the mode of the procedure in trials.[21] For example, in the earlier Roman stage of judicial procedure the conduct of the proceedings was oral. It was known as the *actio legis*. It was a ritualistic proceeding before the magistrate. The prescriptions for this process were given partly by the statutory law, and partly by the group of lawyers whose duty it was to interpret the statutory enactments.

It is uncertain whether for their legal existence private *collegia* needed a civil juridical authorization during the period of the Republic. It does not appear that they had a corporate character. These groups had certainly no power to institute an action in court under the *legis actio* system, since during this period procedural representation was not known.[22]

The Roman formulary system, during the period of the Republic, existed for a time side by side with the *actio legis*. It later superseded the latter as an obligatory form.[23] The formulary proceeding, in the Classical Law Period, was composed of two parts. There was a preliminary hearing before the magistrate (proceeding *in iure*) through whose jurisdictional power the form of the issue in the case was determined. Once this was established the case went before the judge (proceeding *apud iudicem*), and this completed the second phase of the trial.[24]

The trial, in the procedural legislation of Justinian, was consummated in a single forum before a judge who was a state officer subject to public law.[25]

The *Digest*, one of the authentic collections of Justinian, was published in the year 533. This work constituted a reduction of the

[21] Wenger, *Institutes of the Roman Law of Civil Procedure*, translated by Otto Fisk (rev. ed., New York: Veritas Press, 1940), p. 20 (hereafter cited as *Institutes*).

[22] William Smith, *Dictionary of Greek and Roman Antiquities*, I, 470, ad v. "collegium"; Buckland, *A Text-Book of Roman Law* (2. ed., Cambridge: University Press, 1932), p. 177.

[23] Wenger, *Institutes*, p. 23.

[24] Wenger, *Institutes*, p. 24.

[25] Jolowicz, *Historical Introduction to the Study of Roman Law* (Cambridge: University Press, 1932), p. 402. Wenger, *Institutes*, p. 255.

copious juristic literature to an orderly pattern. The juristic literature was the substantial development of early statutory and edictal law. The *Digest* contains the so-called *dicta prudentum* of Gaius, Papinianus, Paulus, Ulpianus, Modestinus and other noted jurists of the second and third centuries.[26] It is in this collection of Justinian (527-565) that the method of procedure for private corporate bodies is to be found. Persons who were allowed to form corporations under a decree of the senate, or through a constitution of the emperor, were considered similar to a municipality, and so became entitled to have common property, a common treasury and an agent or syndic.[27] A corporation, having neither body or soul, could not act except through some representative or agent.

A corporation, in Roman Law, could sue or be sued in a court of justice. It acted through its proper officer.[28] Since the corporate body was considered as a *subiectum iuris,* and hence as capable of having rights and duties, it follows as a necessary corollary that these rights and duties had to be protected and defended in law before lawfully constituted tribunals.

ARTICLE 3. PROCEDURAL REPRESENTATION FOR CORPORATE PERSONS

The central point of the sphere of action especially created for corporate bodies is the procedural representation. It is of the essential marks of the Roman *universitas,* which was recognized as a subject of law, that it had received the capacity to act effectively through an *actor, syndicus* or *defensor.*

In some places in Roman Law the term *actor* was used in designation of the procedural representative of corporate bodies,[29] while in another place the term *syndicus* was used.[30] However, in an at-

[26] Van Hove, *Commentarium Loveniense in Codicem Iuris Canonici,* Vol. I, Tom. I, *Prolegomena ad Codicem Iuris Canonici* (2. ed., Melchliniae—Romae: H. Dessain, 1945), p. 214 (hereafter cited *Prolegomena*).

[27] D. (3, 4) (1, 1). This carries the heading: *Gaius libro tertio ad edictum provinciale.* Gaius lived in the second century.

[28] D. (3, 4) 7; D. (2, 4) (10, 4); D. (3, 4) (1, 1).

[29] D. (2, 4) (10, 4); D. (3, 4) (1, 1); D. (3, 4) 2; D. (3, 4) 10.

[30] D. (3, 4) (1, 1). Bouix (1808-1870) stated that in more recent parlance the name *syndicus* was reserved for procurators who were deputed or delegated by colleges properly so called.—*Tractatus de Judiciis Ecclesiasticis* (2. ed., 2 vols., Parisiis, 1855), I, 224.

tempt to find a reason for the existence of these two terms in Roman Law and the distinction, if any, between them, it can be stated that according to some authorities the term *actor* was to be understood, in general, of one designated for procedural representation in an individual case. These authorities based their opinion on the *Digest* citation mentioned.[31]

There is some evidence that the term *syndicus,* appearing only in the second century, had the meaning of a legal adviser or lawyer in some definite process.[32] At a later time the word appeared in the meaning of a representative similar to a procurator, as we now know it, in a concrete procedural affair.[33] One authority maintains that for all practical purposes there was no difference in meaning between the terms *actor* and *syndicus.*[34]

On the other hand, for a more complete understanding of the use of these terms one should attend to the opinion of Gierke in this matter. He was inclined to the belief that it is uncertain whether, with reference to the passage of the *Digest* under discussion, the term *syndicus* and *actor* were used, the one to designate persons representing the corporation in all cases, and the other to designate persons representing it in some particular case, so that there existed for each term a crystallized meaning as created by such a technical distinction.[35]

The term *defensor* had also been used in the sources of Roman Law to designate a representative of the corporate body. In the fourth century the word seemed to denote someone in the employ of the state whose duty it was to represent a party in a judicial

---

[31] D. (3, 4).

[32] Philostratus, *Vitae Sophistarum,* I, 25; English translation by Wright (Loeb Classical Library), pp. 126 ff.

[33] C (1, 3) (17, 1).

[34] Schnorr von Carolsfeld, *Geschichte der juristischen Person,* Vol. 1, (München: Beck, 1933), p. 325. Cf. Lenel, "E. Albertario, 'Syndicus' *BIDR,* XXVII, 87, 1914, *Zeitschrift der Savigny-Stiftung für Rechtsgeschichte,* Romanistische Abteilung, XLIV (1924), 550.

[35] Gierke, *Das deutsche Genossenschaftsrecht* (4 vols., Berlin: Weidmannsche Buchhandlung, 1881-1913), III, 165, fn. 133 (hereafted cited *Genossenschaftsrecht*).

cause.[36] The Greeks used the word *syndicus* to designate the party who was such a *defensor* or public defender.[37]

So, finally, regardless of whether the representatives of these corporate beings were termed *actores* or *syndici,* they possessed, in the final analysis, the same rights as an ordinary procurator.[38] If the entire corporate body was reduced to a single member, even an individual possessing one of the offices aforementioned, the better opinion was that he could sue and be sued, since the right of all was merged in one, provided that the suit was brought or defended under the corporate title. The same principle held for the *defensor.*[39]

In the Classical Law Period these representatives were appointed *ad hoc.* In later procedure the *syndicus* was a permanent representative for the business affairs of the corporate body and represented it in trials.[40] There were rules which determined the manner of appointing the syndic. The appointment had to be in accord with the statutes or the by-laws of the corporation.

It was necessary for the corporate body to be represented in court by a syndic or some other representative. If the syndic was absent, ill or otherwise incapable of representing the corporation in court, it was deeded that the corporation did not have a representative. The consequence of this was that upon failure of the corporation to respond to the suit the court would order the sale of the corporate property.[41]

The syndic represented the corporation as such, and not the individual members or the several persons composing it, as if they were joint plaintiffs or defendants.[42] Only the syndic, authorized by a vote of the members, could legally institute a suit for the corpora-

---

[36] Schnorr von Carolsfeld, *op. cit.,* I, 326.

[37] Gierke, *op. cit.,* III, 165.

[38] D. (3, 4) 10.

[39] D. (3, 4) (1,3).

[40] D. (3, 4) (1, 1).

[41] D. (3, 4) (1, 2): "Quodsi nemo eos defendat, quod eorum commune erit possideri et, si admoniti non excitentur ad sui defensionem, venire se iussurum proconsul ait. Et quidem non esse actorem vel syndicum tunc quoque intelligimus, cum is absit aut valetudine impedietur aut inhabilis sit ad agendum."

[42] D. (3, 4) 2.

tion.[43] A two-third's vote of the members was required for the election of the representative. To constitute a two-third's part of the membership, the person elected could be included.[44] In an election a son could vote for his father, or the father could vote for his son.[45]

If the corporate body elected someone and shared with him power to appoint a representative for legal proceedings, the representative thus selected was considered as if he had been elected by the entire group.[46]

A syndic, when once appointed to act, held office as the representative of the moral person as long as it so willed. He could be prevented from acting by means of the corporation's resolution to the contrary, or he could also be barred by means of a judicial exception raised against him.[47]

An agent, when empowered to represent a corporate body, was presumed by the court to have been duly appointed and thus stood acknowledged as the proper agent to handle the case. If for any reason some doubt arose as to his appointment, the agent was required to place a bond with the court by way of security for his acts in the trial. The syndic had no right of judicial action for the execution of an edict, unless he in some way had a personal interest in the case.[48]

ARTICLE 4. LEGAL REMEDIES APPLICABLE TO COLLEGIATE BODIES

In Roman Law the corporation was capable of contracting obligations in favor of itself, and also against itself. In consequence of this it was permissible for the corporation to sue or to be sued on a contract duly executed by it.[49]

An action in court on simple contract debts when such a suit was occasioned in view of a loan in favor of the corporate body,

---

[43] D. (3, 4) 3.
[44] D. (3, 4) 4.
[45] D. (3, 4) 5.
[46] D. (3, 4) (6, 1).
[47] D. (3, 4) (6, 2).
[48] D. (3, 4) (6, 3).
[49] Girard, *Manuel Elémentaire de Droit Romain* (7. ed., Paris: Rousseau, 1924), p. 238, Bk. II, ch. 6, 2. Cf. D. (3, 4) (7, 1).

could be asserted against that legal entity only to the extent that the loan had been expended for its benefit.[50]

Execution could be levied against a corporation as upon a natural or physical person by the sale of the corporate property, concursus and by the marshalling of the other assets.[51]

By way of analogy it was presumed that corporate bodies took judicial oaths when oaths were taken by their legal representatives.[52] There appears to be a certain anomaly in this, since the taking of an oath is a personal matter and involves conscience; yet, since the oath could be taken by the representative, it was held as attachable to the corporate body.

Generally considered, a corporation could not be guilty of a crime. There obviously were certain crimes which it could not commit on the very basis of impossibility, for example, adultery or bigamy. It was likewise impossible to transport a corporation, or to imprison a moral person. There could be a deprivation of the corporate charter, which act implied the civil death of the corporate body. But, the capacity to commit crimes, and consequently the subjection to penalties, were factors applicable only to natural persons who were capable of violition and knowledge. Since the moral person lacked this natural ability, no crime could be imputed to it. The crime was rather to be considered as having been committed by one or more of the members of the corporate body in their private capacity.[53]

A *delictum,* in its strict sense, gave rise to an obligation to pay a penalty. This is to be distinguished from the obligation or liability concommitant with the delict, namely, to compensate for the injury done. The former is the effect of the criminal offense: the latter is the effect of the civil tort.[54] The corporation was held liable for its tortious acts. It was held responsible or liable not so much because its agent, in acting for and on its behalf, had done wrong in

---

[50] D. (12, 1) 27.

[51] Colquhoun, *Roman Civil Law* (3 vols., London: Benning, 1849), I, 663.

[52] D. (35, 1) 97: "Municipibus, si iurassent, legatum est. Haec conditio non est impossibilis. *Paulus.* Quemadmodum ergo pareri potest per eos. Itaque iurabunt, per quos municipii res geruntur."

[53] Colquhoun, *op. cit.,* I, 663.

[54] Buckland, *A Manual of Roman Private Law,* p. 317.

the strict sense of a crime, but because he had done harm. It was simply held responsible for damages, though in fact there could be no imputed blame. In all delicts, properly so called, there was a moral element—the *dolus,* and this could not be imputed to a corporation.[55]

The *interdictum de vi* would issue against a municipality for ejectment.[56]

Restitutio in integrum was granted in the *actio quod metus causa* when one had been forced into a transaction by threats. The corporation could be summoned as a defendant in such a suit when its agent was responsible for the threats.[57]

---

[55] Colquhoun, *op. cit.,* I, 664.

[56] D. (43, 16) 4.

[57] Colquhoun, *op. cit.,* I, 665.

CHAPTER III

THE COLLEGIATE MORAL PERSON IN TRIALS FROM THE DECRETALS OF GREGORY IX TO THE PRESENT CODE

Generally taken, the substantive law of any legal system defines the rights which men have and the duties which they owe to others. The adjective law of any legal system determines the remedies or the mode by which men's rights and duties are enforced and protected. However, there are many rights which belong to the realm of the procedural law, such as the right to lodge an appeal or the right to institute a new trial. The adjective law is known as the procedural law. It includes contentious and criminal legal proceedings.

Before one can effectively resort to the final compulsory processes for the enforcement of rights it is necessary to have facts which establish a right. The concern of the present conspectus is not so much with the substantive rights of the collegiate moral persons, as with the trial or process of litigation by means of which their rights could be vindicated. The procedural right of collegiate persons may be considered as a substantive right or as a procedural one. It may be considered as a substantive right, if it be viewed from the standpoint of the moral person's right to sue and to be sued. If it be viewed, however, from the point of the court's right to recognize such a person in a trial and to permit it to sue, it becomes a jurisdictional question, and then it eventuates as a procedural right.

The beginning of the second epoch (XII-XVI centuries) in the history of the collections of Canon Law received a stimulating influence from the *Decretum* of Gratian. The date of Gratian's birth and death are unknown. It is certain only that he died before the years 1157-1159.[1] Van Hove states that the *Decretum* was written about the year 1140.[2] While this work had great influence

[1] Van Hove, *Prolegomena,* p. 339.
[2] *Loc. cit.*

on subsequent canonical legislation, it was nevertheless only a compilation of the old laws. Since it was not an authentic collection of laws, the procedural legislation found therein had only the legal force of the individual laws which composed it.

The first authentic and complete compilation of laws concerning remedial procedure is that found in the Decretals of Gregory IX (1227-1241). The completeness of this legislation restrained subsequent Popes, particularly Boniface VIII (1294-1303) and Clement V (1305-1314), from introducing more than a few additional provisions in their collections.[3] The Decretals remained, in effect, the main source of the procedural rights of collegiate moral persons until the promulgation of the Code. This is evident from the pre-Code commentaries which followed the order which had been observed in them.[4]

The order of the present historical survey of the canonical procedural rights of moral persons will be systematic rather than chronological. Practical controversies will be treated, at least summarily, but the speculative ones, for clear and obvious reasons, will be foregone.

ARTICLE 1. PROCEDURAL CAPACITY

A. *The Person Itself*

Juridical capacity may be expressed in the Latin phrase *iura habere.* Procedural capacity is summed up in the Latin expression *iura libere exercere.*[5] Procedural capacity then is an external, rather than an internal, quality referring to the exercise of the right to sue. Moral persons, such as collegiate or cathedral churches and

---

[3] Wernz-Vidal, *Ius Canonicum,* VI, n. 2, p. 6.

[4] Schmalzgrueber (1663-1735), *Ius Canonicum Universum* (5 vols. in 12, Romae: 1843-1845), lib. III, tit. 1, nos. 39-43 (hereafter this work will be cited simply by the decretalist's name); Reiffenstuel (1642-1703), *Jus Canonicum Universum* (5 vols. in 7, Parisiis, 1864-1870), lib. II, n. 177 (hereafter cited merely by the decretalist's name).

[5] Sipos, *Enchiridion Iuris Canonici* (3. ed. Pecs: *Ex Typographia "Haladás R. T."* 1936), p. 864.

monasteries in the Middle Ages,[6] in their efforts to act procedurally, provided the general basis for the development of our present day understanding of the procedural capacity of collegiate moral persons.

Since the church and the monastery each had juridical capacity in that they were capable (*capaces*) of possessing rights, such as acquiring and possessing goods,[7] these bodies could have their rights protected by the law in the process known as litigation, whether the moral person was a plaintiff or a defendant.[8] But, while it is true that these bodies did have juridical capacity, it is beyond question, during the period under discussion, that the ecclesiastical moral person as such could not exercise a procedural right. This was true because the body considered in itself was a mere creation of ecclesiastical law, and hence by its very nature required a real or physical person to act for it. Therefore it could not, by itself, act in a trial, nor could it initiate a suit or respond to it.[9] Though the trial concerned the corporate body, whether in the nature of plaintiff or of defendant, this body could act only through another, and not personally. Still the trial as a cause which was subject to a judicial hearing pertained to it, for the complaint (*libellus*) was drawn up in its name. So likewise the judgment and the execution were to be referred to it, and not to the representative or even to the members jointly.[10]

---

[6] Nicolaus de Tudeschis (Abbas Panormitanus, 1386-1453), *Commentaria in Quinque Libros Decretalium* (5 vols. in 7, Venetiis, 1588), lib. I, tit. 5, *de rescriptis,* c. 21 (hereafter this work will be cited as Panormitanus).

[7] C. 15, C. XII, p. 1. Friedberg (1837-1910) stated that this canon was derived from the pseudo-Isidorian collection.

[8] Gillet, *La Personalité Juridique en Droit Ecclésiastique* (Malines: W. Godène, 1927), p. 120 (hereafter cited *La Personalité Juridique*).

[9] Innocentius IV (Sinibaldus Fliscus, d. 1254), *Apparatus* (*Commentaria*) *in Libros Quinque Decretalium* (Venetiis: de Colonia et Jenson, 1481), lib. II, tit. 1, c. 14, ad v. "indiscrete" (This work is to be found in the Library of Congress. Hereafter it will be cited as *Commentaria.*) : "Universitas per se agere non potest nec narrare nec respondere." *Glossa ordinaria* of c. 1, II, 1, in VI°, ad v. "delegatum": "In causis vero ecclesiae, collegii vel universitatis de necessitate intervenit syndicus." C. 16, X, *de iudiciis,* II, 1; Potthast, *Regesta Pontificum Romanorum inde ab. A. post Christum natum MCXCVIII ad A. MDCCCIV* (2 vols., Berolini, 1874-1875), n. 2740 (hereafter cited Potthast). Cf. c. 14, X, *de iudiciis,* II, 1, ad v. "proponant."

[10] Gierke, *Genossenschaftsrecht,* III, 339.

B. *Representative Procedural Rights of Abbots, Prelates and Inferiors*

The term "prelate," as used herein, denotes one who had episcopal jurisdiction in some church in which there was a chapter (*capitulum*). The term "abbot," as used herein, points to the primary prelate of a religious order and to a superior general.[11]

By apostolic authority Innocent III (1198-1216) forbade secular judges, as well as ecclesiastical judges, to deny to a certain preceptor of the Knights Templar the right of prosecuting and defending the cases of the moral person whom he represented. The preceptor had been denied the procedural right to sue in these courts on various pretexts, such as the failure to allege a free status.[12] The gloss to this canon exemplified the principle that there was a presumption of freedom or capacity to sue in these persons.[13] And this presumption was said to arise from the dignity which these preceptors had.[14]

In the year 1208 Innocent III replied to a letter from the Canons Regular of Premontré. He answered the question which was submitted to him concerning the procedural right of an abbot, cited in a cause of the monastery, when no mention was made of the community or convent. It was held sufficient to cite merely the abbot without any need of mentioning the community. This decision was based on the fact that *ex officio* the abbot had the obligation of tending to the affairs of the monastery, and thus was the proper party to be cited. Innocent further advised that this ruling would not hold if the goods or rights of the abbot and the community were entirely separate or distinct.[15]

Panormitanus could not understand how the goods of the monastery could be separate from the abbot's unless the mensal support of the abbot was distinct from that of the chapter.[16] The Glossator further explained the right of the abbot[17] as the repre-

---

[11] C. 1, *de rescriptis,* I, 2, in Clem.; Bouix, *Tractatus de Judiciis Ecclesiasticis,* I, p. 181, n. XII.

[12] C. 16, X, *de iudiciis,* II, 1.

[13] *Glossa ordinaria* of c. 16, X, *de iudiciis,* II, 1, ad v. "nationis."

[14] *Loc. cit.*

[15] C. 21, X, *de rescriptis,* I, 3; Potthast, n. 3305.

[16] Lib. I, tit. 5, *de rescriptis,* c. 21.

[17] *Glossa ordinaria* of c. 21, X, *de rescriptis,* I, 3, ad v. "debeant."

sentative of the monastery in that he commended the procedure of bringing suit against the abbot, rather than against the community, for thus there was avoided the delay that would have been needed for the naming and the substituting of the abbot in the cause.[18] If the judicial action had proceeded to a final determination against the moral person as such without naming the abbot, the sentence could have been set aside, since it was not possible for the moral person to sue or be sued without the consent of the abbot.

The Council of Tarragona (516) and the IX Council of Toledo (655) had both held that monks generally could not act in temporal affairs without the consent and the approval of the abbot.[19] The real guardianship vested in the abbot over the monks was similar to the Roman concept of the parental authority of the father over his son. The Gloss explained, therefore, that a community or a convent should not sue or respond to a suit without the consent of the abbot. The abbot, on the other hand, should not sue without the consent of the community. The same rule was applied to the prelate in relation to his chapter. The abbot or prelate was to appoint a syndic or a procurator for the trial itself, unless the matter concerned the community or the chapter particularly, and then it, with the consent of the abbot or the prelate, could appoint the procedural representative.

If the office of abbot or prelate was vacant, no suits were to be opened or defended during the interim; but, if the community or the chapter had acted during the vacancy, then a subsequent approval or ratification was sufficient.[20] The Glossator based his opinion, in which he asserted the need of consent from both the abbot and the community for either's choice of a representative authorized to sue or to respond in court, on the ground that neither of them could alienate the moral person's property without the consent of both, and therefore neither could alone jeopardize the corporate rights in a trial without a special permission of the other.[21] The

[18] Cf. c. 5, X, *ut lite non contestata non procedatur ad testium receptionem vel ad sententiam diffinitivam,* II, 6; Potthast, n. 3665.

[19] C. 35, C. XVI, p. 1; Bruns, *Canones Apostolorum et Conciliorum Saeculorum IV-VII* (2 vols. Berolini, Reimeri, 1839) II, 17 (hereafter cited as Bruns); c. 10, C. XVI, p. 3; Bruns, I, 294.

[20] *Glossa ordinaria* of c. 21, X, *de rescriptis,* I, 3, ad v. "debeant."

[21] *Glossa ordinaria* of c. 21, X, *de rescriptis,* I, 3, ad v. "debeant."

conclusion of the Glossator was, therefore, that the consent of the community or of the chapter was always needed for the abbot or the prelate to lodge a suit or to respond to it in defense of the collegiate moral person in court.[22]

The Gloss further considered what was to be done if a judicial controversy arose between the abbot and the monastery. In that instance an approach was to be made to a superior for the appointment of a curator for the *collegium* or the moral body, and such a curator would then represent it in the court, his office terminating at the end of the trial. Of course, if the convent or the chapter did not desire a *curator ad litem,* it could have a procurator appointed.

Whether the abbot of a monastery or the prelate of a cathedral church could initiate a suit or respond to it without the respective consent of the community or of the chapter remained for a long period a controverted question among the canonists.[23] Some canonists argued that such a consent was always necessary, since the Gloss to the decretal letter of Innocent III,[24] as well as the Gloss to a letter written by Gregory the Great in 602 to the Bishop of Salona,[25] required the consent of either the community or the chapter. There were many prescriptions on the alienation of church property which seemed to add weight to this opinion.[26]

However, the more common opinion, as held by Pirhing (1606-1679), Reiffenstuel (1642-1703), Schmalzgrueber (1663-1735) and others, upheld the opposite position. The decretalists almost commonly were of the opinion that, as a general rule, the abbot or

---

[22] *Loc. cit.;* c. 1, X, *de procuratoribus,* I, 28. Cf. the *Glossa ordinaria* to this canon ad v. "legaliter"; Jaffé, *Regesta Pontificum Romanorum, ab condita ecclesia ad annum post Christum natum MCXCVIII* (2. ed., correctam et auctam auspiciis Gulielmi Wattenbach, curaverunt S. Loewenfeld, F. Kaltenbrunner, P. Ewald, 2 vols. in 1, Lipsiae, 1885-1888), JE, n. 1874 (hereafter cited JL, JK, JE). Cf. also the whole of title XIII, *de rebus ecclesiae aliendis vel non,* in the third book of the Decretals of Gregory IX.

[23] Gierke, *Genossenschaftsrecht,* III, 339.

[24] *Glossa ordinaria* of c. 21, X, *de rescriptis,* I, 3, ad v. "debeant."

[25] *Glossa ordinaria* of c. 1, X, *de procuratoribus,* I, 28, ad v. "legaliter"; JE, n. 1874.

[26] Cf. the whole of title XIII, *de rebus ecclesiae aliendis vel non,* in the third book of the Decretals of Gregory IX.

the prelate did not need the respective consent of the community or of the chapter to act for the collegiate moral person in trials.[27] These canonists based their opinion on the ground that the abbot and the prelate had the free administration of the moral person's affairs and that, since there was no restriction in the law on their right to act in a representative's capacity, no restriction was to be implied. The term representative was understood in a broad meaning. The representative had all the rights which the common law, the particular law, the constitutions and current usages attributed to him.[28]

The possession of these rights in their entirety on the part of the representative was not acknowledged by the canonists if the matter was of great moment, or if the consent was required in a particular case wherein the administration of the affairs of the moral person was common to both the abbot and the monastery. In this case the abbot needed the consent of the community to initiate a suit or to defend a judicial cause. This same rule held for prelates in relation to cathedral or collegiate chapters.[29]

The superior of a religious house, if he was not an abbot, could or could not act for the moral person over which he presided, depending on the rights conferred on him by the general constitutions of the institute or the customary usages.[30]

The superioress of a convent of nuns could be plaintiff or de-

---

[27] Schmalzgrueber, lib. II, tit. 1, n. 39; Pirhing, *Jus Canonicum in Quinque Libros Decretalium Distributum* (5 vols., Dilingae, 1674-1678), lib. II, tit. 1, n. 24 (hereafter cited as Pirhing); Schmier, *Iurisprudentia Canonico-Civilis* (2 vols., Venetiis, 1754), lib. II, tract, 1, c. 2, n. 149 (hereafter cited Schmier); Reiffenstuel, lib. I, tit. 1, n. 172; Gonzalez-Tellez, *Commentaria Perpetua in singulos textus quinque librorum Decretalium Gregorii IX* (5 vols., 1699), lib. I, tit. 3, c. 21 (hereafter cited as Gonzalez-Tellez); Barbosa, *Collectanea Doctorum tam Veterum quam Recentiorum in Jus Pontificum Universum* (2 vols., Lugduni, 1716), lib. I, tit. 3, c. 21 (hereafter cited as Barbosa).

[28] Panormitanus (lib. I, tit. 5, *de rescriptis,* c. 21) stated that the "*rector alicuius universitatis*" could by and of himself act in the affairs of the whole community.

[29] Pirhing, lib. II, tit. 1, n. 24; Schmier, lib. II, tract 1, c. 2, n. 152.

[30] Schmalzgrueber, lib. II, tit. 1, n. 40.

fendant in a judicial cause for the convent through a duly constituted procurator.[31]

The prelate did not have the right to open a suit in court or to defend it in a cause which was proper to the chapter, unless he had obtained from the chapter a special mandate to proceed with the cause. If he had acted without this mandate, the chapter later had to ratify his actions.[32] This law followed the principle, *"Quod omnes tangit, debet ab omnibus approbari."*[33]

Although everyone was free to exercise his natural right as prospective plaintiff or defendant, the abbot or prelate and other similar superiors of moral bodies could not, for the simple reason that *ex officio* the administration of the corporate affairs was committed to them, exercise the option of foregoing court procedure if the use of this option begot prejudicial consequences for the moral body in whose name they acted. Such superiors could be compelled to resort to action in court.[34]

C. *The Rights of the Community or the Chapter*

If the administration of certain goods was attributable not merely to the abbot or prelate but in a specific way to a chapter or a community, then these groups were to exercise their full rights as plaintiffs and defendants in all such corporate matters.[35] In cases wherein the matter under consideration was of an arduous character or of great moment for the moral body, the community or the chapter could not propose a suit or defend it in court without the consent of the abbot or the prelate.[36] If the community or the chapter acted in a cause that was proper to the abbot or the prelate, it acted

[31] C. un., *de statu regularium,* III, 16, in VI°; Schmalzgrueber, lib. II, tit. 1, n. 40; c. 2, X, *de his, quae fiunt a praelato sine consensu capituli,* III, 10, ad v. "continebatur."

[32] *Glossa ordinaria* of c. 1, X, *de procuratoribus,* I, 38 ,ad v. "legaliter"; JE, n. 1874; Schmalzgrueber, lib. II, tit. 1, n. 43; Pirhing, lib. II, tit. 1, n. 24.

[33] Reg. 29, R.J., in VI°.

[34] Bouix, *Tractatus de Judiciis Ecclesiasticis,* I, 183.

[35] Schmalzgrueber, lib. II, tit. 1, n. 39; Ioannes Andreae, *In Quinque Decretalium Libros Novella Commentaria* (4 vols., Venetiis, 1581), lib. II, tit. 1, c. 9, n. 4; Pirhing, lib. II, tit. 1, n. 26.

[36] Schmalzgrueber, lib. II, tit. 1, n. 39; Pirhing, lib. II, tit, 1, n. 24.

illegally without a special mandate from the latter. The acts which were undertaken without such a special mandate had later to be ratified by the respective superior.[37]

Before the Code, then, canonists proposed the general question whether a prelate of seculars (for example, the bishop in relation to the cathedral church or cathedral chapter) or a prelate of regulars (abbots, superiors general, etc.), could stand in trial without the consent of the chapter or the convent. In practice three cases were distinguished: 1) the goods (i.e., the properties) were held in common by the prelate and the chapter; 2) the goods were held separately, but their administration was held in common; and, 3) both the goods and the administration were held separately by the superior and the community.

With reference to the first and second cases canonists held that the prelate or abbot could stand in trial for the moral body without the consent of the chapter, unless the cause was *"ardua et magni praeiudicii."* This rule was based on the general principle that whosoever had been constituted as universal procurator for the affairs of the moral body was able to act (*agere*) without a special mandate, save for those cases which were expressly excepted in the law. The *"causa ardua"* was explicitly singled out in the Decretals as an excepted case.[38]

On the contrary, the chapter or the convent was never able to stand in court in these cases without the consent of the prelate, for a prelate was *ex officio suo* bound to oversee the affairs of his community.[39] Only one case was excepted from this rule. If upon an act of wrongful alienation of property a prelate or his successor had neglected to demand restitution, then some member of the chapter was conceded to be competent for the act of raising the issue in court.[40]

With reference to the third case the chapter or the convent was able to stand in court without the consent of the prelate, unless the issue regarding its separate goods or administration constituted a

---

[37] *Glossa ordinaria* of c. 1, X, *de procuratoribus,* I, 35, ad v. "legaliter"; Schmalzgrueber, lib. II, tit, 1, nn. 42, 43; Pirhing, lib. II, tit, 1, n. 28.

[38] Cc. 1, 3, 8, 9, X, *de his, quae fiunt a praelato sine consensu capituli,* III, 10.

[39] Reiffenstuel, lib. II, tit. 1, n. 177.

[40] C. 6, X, *de his, quae fiunt a praelato sine consensu capituli,* III, 10.

causa magnique praeiudicii. This limitation was deduced analogously: just as the prelate could not without the consent of the chapter stand in court when the cause was particularly intricate, so neither could the chapter if it lacked the consent of the prelate.[41]

In practice, however, the prelates, rectors and administrators of moral persons were subjected to many limitations not only by the common law,[42] the particular law, and current usages, but also by the particular constitutions of the various corporate bodies.

ARTICLE 2. THE CRIMINAL PROCEEDINGS

In the historical sources of pre-Code law divergent views were expressed on the question whether in the ecclesiastical forum a collegiate moral person was a subject capable of a delictual act. This question remained controverted even to modern times.[43] There is some evidence that the corporate body in and of itself was not held accountable in the matter of criminal acts.[44] At the beginning of his observations, Innocent IV held the opionion that the law did not hold the moral being liable for any criminal conduct, since the being as such was incapable of committing a crime.[45]

Some authors hold that this opinion necessarily followed from the adherence to the canonical fiction theory regarding corporate bodies. According to Gierke, the first man to use the term "*persona ficta*" was Sinibald Fieschi, Pope Innocent IV.[46] But the modern canonical authors disagree with Gierke's view by attributing to

---

[41] Reiffenstuel, lib. II, tit. 1, nn. 180, 181.

[42] This can be seen from the relatively large number of chapters in Title 10, *de his, quae fiunt a praelato sine consensu capituli,* in Book III of the Decretals of Gregory IX.

[43] Wernz, *Ius Decretalium,* VI, n. 18: "Utrum sola persona individua an etiam corporationes (universitates), quae pluribus personis singularibus constant, sint in foro ecclesiastico subiecta capacia delictorum in controversia est."

[44] Cf. *Glossa ordinaria* of c. 58, C. 12, q. 2, ad v. "accusandi," where it is stated that the word *accusandi* pointed simply to a civil inquisition or to an accusation against either a bishop or the individual members of the chapter, since the corporate body *"non potest de crimine accusari."*

[45] *Commentaria,* lib. V., tit. 39, c. 53, ad v. "consiliaros": ". . . impossibile est quod universitas delinquat." Cf. Durandus, *Speculum Juris* (3 vols., Venetiis, 1577), lib. IV, pars 4, *de sententia excommunicationis,* n. 4—"quia universitas non habet animam . . . unde nec delinquat nec punitur."

[46] Gierke, *Genossenschaftsrecht,* III, 279.

Innocent not the fictiona theory but rather the realist theory.[47] However, for the purpose of the present dissertation the important factor to stress is that the collegiate moral person has a *juridical* personality. Whether this personality is a *verum et distinctum iuris subietum,* as the fiction theory maintains, or whether it is an ontological reality resulting from the group of individuals who are so united that from many persons there develops one legal person, as the realists maintain, the writer will not discuss. For in both theories a juridical personality results, and what concerns the corporate body will not concern the members as individuals.[48]

Innocent IV and the canonists did develop the idea of corporate personality, based on that of the Roman corporation, although they lived in a Germanic legal environment, which had for its practical basis the collegiate or cathedral church.[49] Innocent held, and not without warrant in the *Digest* for his opinion,[50] that the ecclesiastical corporation could not in its corporate nature commit a sin or a crime. And as legislator the Pope did consider a collegiate moral person free from subjection to any ecclesiastical penalty such as excommunication, for he prohibited the inflicting of a sentence of excommunication upon a corporate body.[51] Innocent and numerous other canonists justified this prohibition on the ground that the juridic person was a being without a soul and without baptism. Furthermore, a transfer of the effect of excommunication to all the individuals composing the corporate body would have effected the souls of the innocent along with those of the guilty.[52] But the

---

[47] Wernz, op. cit., VI, n. 18. Brown, *Juristic Personality,* pp. 52-60.

[48] *Loc. cit.*

[49] Gierke, *Genossenschaftsrecht,* III, 279; Harold J. Laski, "The Early History of the Corporation in England" 30 *Harvard Law Review* 561-588. This author, in a footnote *ibid.,* p. 575, said: "Cf. H. A. Smith, *Law of Associations,* 152-157. He [Smith] seems to me [Laski] to have shown good grounds for doubting Dr. Gierke's picture of Innocent as a great speculative lawyer." But this opinion of Laski is decidedly against the generally accepted thought among the canonical authors.

[50] D. (4, 3) (15, 1).

[51] C. 5, V, *de sententia excommunicationis,* XI, in VI°. Gierke, *Genossenschaftsrecht,* III, 280.

[52] Panormitanus, lib. V, tit. 3, *de simonia,* c. 30, n. 12: "excommunicatio . . . requirit verum corpus et animam baptizatam et verum et proprium delictum excommunicandi." Panormitanus, lib. III, tit. 49, c. 7, nn. 8, 22. Hostiensis, *Summa Aurea* (Basileae, 1573), lib. V, tit. 39, n. 6.

question remains whether Innocent convinced his fellow lawyers that the corporate person could never be responsible for a crime or a tort.

During the Middle Ages the idea of criminal responsibility of associations in general became deep-rooted in the social consciousness of the times. It was reflected in the civil (state) legislation and in the secular legal practice.[53] The canonists seemed to have no alternative but to modify their theory regarding the possibility of crime on the part of a corporation, in order to harmonize their teaching with the trend of the social development of the times. Popular conviction regarding an association's responsibility for delicts or crimes was so deep-rooted that the canonists were unable to ignore it even in the light of their own logical conclusions to the contrary in regard to the corporate body in ecclesiastical law.[54] Later commentators, at least occasionally, mentioned the axiom, "*impossibile est quod universitas delinquat,*"[55] but the majority of the canonists expressly held the opposite opinion, namely, *universitas et ecclesia delinquere possunt,* and one could even produce a canon which spoke of a spiritual crime of fornication and adultery on the part of a church when it relinquished its episcopal shepherd in exchange for another.[56] The social thought was, perhaps, of far inferior caliber alongside the philosophical and classical Innocentian doctrine But in spite of this deficiency, it so affected the practical angles of corporation law, that canonists felt themselves under compulsion to subscribe to the new view. Innocent IV, while writing his *Commentaria,* seemed fully aware of the contrary trend. For the way of thinking of the majority made it seem easier to attach responsibility to a corporation or *universitas* as an in-

[53] Gierke, *Genossenschaftsrecht,* III, 343.

[54] Gierke, *Genossenschaftsrecht,* III, 343.

[55] *Glossa ordinaria* of c. 30, X, *de simonia et ne aliquid pro spiritualibus exigatur vel promittatur,* V, 3, ad v. "officialibus"; Durandus, *Speculum Juris,* lib. IV, pars 4, n. 4.

[56] C. 11, C. VII, p. 1 (Pseudo-Isidor): "Alterum episcopum vivente suo non accipiat (ecclesia), ne aut fornicationis aut adulterii crimen incurrat." The *Glossa ordinaria* to this canon ad v. "adulterata" stated: "Ergo ecclesia potest delinquere et etiam universitas."

separable unit.[57] Thus the majority aligned its thought with the newly developed trend, which seems attributable to the social forces of the time rather than any change in the philosophical viewpoint.

There were a few canonists who, while denying in principle the capacity of a corporate body to commit crimes, saw themselves forced to make considerable concessions to the new theory. While adhering to the old theory, they had to admit a considerable extension of the principle of representation, so that in regard to the legal consequences of certain illicit actions on the part of physical persons representing the corporation they held that such actions should be imputed to the juristic person.[58] They even admitted the responsibility of the moral person for acts authorized by a majority of its members, as well as, in part, its responsibility for the acts of its representative.[59]

A fortiori, a criminal deed perpetrated or assented to by all the members of a corporate body was treated as the crime or offense of the corporation itself.[60] The collegiate moral person was represented in the criminal trial by the procurator.[61] On the other hand, the criminal acts of the individual members of these bodies, even if they were officers, were as such not imputed to the corporation.[62]

---

[57] Hostiensis, *Summa Aurea,* lib. II, tit. 14, *de dolo,* n. 7. Cf. c. un., *de poenis,* tit. 12, in Extravag. Ioan. XXII, ad vv. "quae dilinquerit": ". . . potest ergo universitas delinquere, licet non de facili, cum de facili non consentiat."

[58] Innocentius IV, *Commentaria,* lib. V, tit. 39, c. 53: "Fatemur, tamen, quod si rectores alicuius universitatis vel alii aliquod maleficium faciunt de mandato universitatis totius vel tantae partis, quod invitis aliis maleficium fecerint, vel etiam sine mandato fecerint, sed postea universitas quod suo nomine erat factum, ratum habet: quod universitas punietur . . ."

[59] *Glossa ordinaria* of c. 56, C. XII, p. 2, ad v. "accusandi": ". . . et delictum, quod maiores de universitate committunt, ad omnes refertur."

[60] Durandus, *Speculum Juris,* lib. I, pars 2 *de accusatore,* par 1, n. 7; *Glossa ordinaria* of c. 2, X, *de ordine cognitionum,* II, 10, ad v. "ipsius dolum."

[61] *Glossa ordinaria* of c. 53, C. XII, q. 2, ad v. "accusandi"; *Glossa ordinaria* of c 5, V, 11, in VI°, ad v. "collegium"; Durandus, *Speculum Juris,* I, pars 3, *de procuratoribus,* par 1, n. 11.

[62] *Glossa ordinaria* of c. 7, C. 16, q. 6: "Episcopo non liceat possessionem monasterii tollere quamvis abbas peccaverit"; Innocentius IV, *Commentaria,* lib. I, tit. 33, c. 8, ad v. "obedientia"; lib. II, tit. 2, c. 7, ad vv. "de feudis."

Those canonists who denied the capacity of a corporation to commit a delict properly so called as imputable to the corporate body as such, at least in the ecclesiastical forum, did not deny that the corporation could be held for its tort or the tort of its representative in a proceeding before the contentious law courts. There, in place of the mere *inquisitio super statu,* the "civil" court could impose fines and spiritual censures.[63]

Spiritual censures should have been completely excluded in regard to corporations, for such penalties were to be invoked solely against individuals. But in ancient times theory and practice were not always in agreement, although later there emerged a very definite distinction in this regard between excommunication and interdict.[64]

The penalty of interdict, along also with that of suspension, in both theory and practice alike could be invoked against corporate bodies. There was a distinction between the interdicts used. One of them was an interdict inflicted upon a territory or region for the delict of the *dominus loci* or other individuals; the other was an interdict inflicted upon the corporate association for its delict, in the sense herein set forth. In the first case the effects were determined territorially. In the second they were determined personally. There could be no effect on the juridic body itself, as such, for *"ista (interdicta) cadunt in animam rationabilem et personam veram, non repraesentatem,"* and the *"divinorum auditio et sacramentorum perceptio populo ut universis non competunt."* The effect of the interdict had therefore to be referred to the individuals who composed the juridic body, *"ne sententia effectu careat."* And thus it was the individual members who suffered the interdict according to the accepted rule: *"Interdicto populo, singulares de*

---

[63] Innocentius IV, *Commentaria,* lib. V, tit. 3, c. 30, ad v. "severitatis": ". . . nos dicimus, quod universitas non potest accusari nec puniri, sed delinquentes tantum. Civiliter autem conveniri et pecuniariter puniri potest ex delicto rectorum. Praeterea potest inquiri super statu universitatis, sed nec tunc puniuntur nisi . . ."; *ibid.,* ad v. "officialibus": ". . . quod ista faciunt vel sciunt vel tolerant." Cf. Gierke, *Genossenschaftsrecht,* III, 346— ". . . geistliche Censuren."

[64] C. 1, C. XXIV, q. 3; *Glossa ordinaria* to c. 58, C XII, q. 2, ad v. "accusandi": ". . . civitas non potest excommunicari." ". . . et videmus quod saepe capitulum accusatur et excommunicatur concilium universitatis."

populo intelliguntur interdicti." The specification of the individuals who suffered the penalties was determined by the fact of their membership in the corporate body.[65]

ARTICLE 3. THE REPRESENTATIVE FOR TRIALS

A. *Nature of the Office*

The abbot of a monastery was commonly held to be the one to initiate a suit in the interest of the moral person and to respond to a suit lest the moral person remain without a judicial defense. In virtue of his office and as a member of the collegiate body he could exercise the procedural rights of the body except in such cases as have been previously pointed out.[66] But when the abbot appeared for his monastery, or a prelate for his church, his appearance was that of an official of the corporation, and not that of a corporate representative in the sense of a procurator. He was apparently an official acting as an agent.[67]

The ecclesiastical corporation, however, did have a procedural representative. He was called a procurator or syndic, and was usually given full power (*plena potestas*) by the members composing the moral persons. In the Decretals of Gregory IX there follows after the title "*de procuratoribus*" the title "*de syndico,*" comprising a single canon. Gregory I (591) had advised that the religious corporate body should appoint a syndic for managing its affairs of business.[68] The syndic was a type of procurator who was

---

[65] Panormitanus, lib. III, tit. 2, nn. 8-9; *Glossa ordinaria,* c. 16, *de sententia excommunicationis,* V, 11, in VI° ad vv. "interdicti" and "non competant"; Innocentius IV, *Commentaria,* lib. V, tit. 39, c. 53; Gierke, *Genossenschaftsrecht,* III, 349.

[66] Gierke, *Genossenschaftsrecht,* III, 339, citing Tancredus, I, 6, par 1, and Hostiensis, *Summa Aurea,* lib. 1, tit. 39, *de syndico,* n. 4.

[67] Dr. Gaines Post, "Roman Law and Early Representation in Spain and Italy, 1150-1250"—*Speculum, A Journal of Mediaeval Studies,* The Mediaeval Academy of America, XVIII (1943), 211-232, esp. p. 214. Cf. Post, "Plena Potestas and Consent in Mediaeval Assemblies"—*Traditio,* I (1943), 369, 386.

[68] C. un., X *de syndico* I, 39; Jaffé, n. 1136.

appointed or constituted by a moral body or corporation, or by its administrator.[69] Sometimes the corporate body had what was known as an *actor* to represent it in trial. The *actor* differed from the *syndicus* in this that he was constituted or appointed by a special decree of the moral person to represent it in a particular case. The syndic, on the other hand, was appointed without such a decree. He was authorized to represent the corporate person in a present controversial issue as well as in future litigation.[70]

There was no particular stress laid on names. Whether a representative was called an *"actor,"* a *"syndicus"* or even an *"oeconomus,"* in all cases he served in the capacity of a procurator. The representative's rights and duties, extensive or limited, depended on the grant in the appointment made by the persons comprising the juridic being.[71]

By granting to the procedural representative the *plena potestas,* or full power, the corporate body in an implied manner, if not expressly, consented to the jurisdiction of the court when exercised over him in any case that would be instituted. And by submitting to this jurisdiction they also bound themselves to any decision rendered according to law. It was generally held by courts that this procedural representative for corporations should have the *plena potestas,* and not merely some limited power.[72]

There is an early instance of a procurator who represented a number of corporate monasteries. He was active in a suit brought against the Archbishop of Ravenna by all the monasteries of Bologna.[73]

---

[69] Wernz-Vidal, *Ius Canonicum,* VI, n. 241, p. 211.

[70] *Loc. cit.,* citing Tancredus.

[71] Innocentius IV, *Commentaria,* lib. I, tit. 38, c. 9, ad v. "actores"; Hostiensis, *Summa Aurea,* lib. I, tit. 38, *de procuratoribus,* n. 1: "Sed secundum iura nostra planum est: quia non facimus vim in nominibus; nam sive dicatur procurator, sive syndicus, sive oeconomus, sive asinus, sive etiam nullum nomen exprimatur, nihil obstat, dummodo de mente constituentis liqueat." Gierke noted that the representative was commonly known as the work horse (*Esel*) of the corporation!—*Genossenschaftsrecht,* III, 341.

[72] Post, "Roman Law and Early Representation in Spain and Italy, 1150-1250"—*Speculum,* XVIII (1943), 211.

[73] C. 14, X, *de censibus, exactionibus et procuratoribus,* III, 39.

B. *The Appointment*

The syndic was appointed by the majority vote of those persons who had the right to appoint such a person. He could of course also be appointed by anyone who by delegation was given the right to appoint him. This principle applied to corporate bodies of both men and women religious.[74] In a criminal proceeding a syndic was to be appointed in the same manner.[75] If for any reason the judge in the trial objected to the representative of the collegiate body, his objection was never to become a factor that would redound to the prejudice of the moral person.[76] If the term of office of the representative expired during a trial, it was disputed whether he could continue to represent the moral person until the conclusion of the trial was reached. Durandus (1238-1296) was of the opinion that such an individual could proceed as a representative in the case to the final determination of the issue.[77]

Objection to the right of the particular representative to stand in court for the collegiate moral body was to be raised before the trial.[78] It was disputed whether in a judicial controversy between the abbot and the monastery the representative of the latter should be appointed by the abbot or by the monastery. Some held that the abbot could appoint a syndic in such a case, but for that trial only. Others maintained that the monastery had the right to appoint the syndic in such circumstances, which right they based on the assumption that the office of superior was vacant.[79]

An abbot could ratify the appointment of a syndic when he had been chosen or elected without the abbot's consent. This ratification could be given before, during or after joinder of issues.[80] The syndic could be appointed for a temporary or a permanent service. He could be given the power to handle all affairs or merely par-

---

[74] Durandus, *Speculum Juris,* lib. I, partic. III, *de syndico,* § 1, n. 4.

[75] *Ibidem,* n. 5.

[76] *Ibidem,* n. 6.

[77] *Ibidem,* n. 8. This rule was also applied to the syndic representing convents of nuns. Cf. *ibidem,* n. 17.

[78] *Ibidem,* n. 9.

[79] *Ibidem,* n. 19.

[80] *Ibidem,* n. 20.

ticular cases. He could be restricted to the handling of judicial proceedings, or to the management of extra-judicial matters.[81]

C. *The Rights and the Duties of the Representative*

The rôle of plaintiff or of defendant was undertaken in the name of the collegiate moral body, and not in the name of the representative, regardless of whether he functioned as an *actor,* a syndic or a procurator.[82] Similarly the judicial procedure could not be carried on in the names of the members of the corporate body jointly.[83]

Once the syndic was appointed he became the representative of the moral body. This principle was based on the fact that the members themselves acted in a representative capacity in appointing him to represent the body.[84] The corporate person was the real person. This person was substituted for the natural persons who had procured its creation. They had an interest in it, for their rights were vested in it, and it was through their rights that a proper control and management was to be effected. But, if the corporate purpose of a moral or juridic body was called in question in a lawsuit, all pleas and all defenses invoked against them had to be undertaken in the corporate name of the collegiate person. The moral person had to undertake its judicial action in a specified manner, through its duly constituted officers or agents, whose acts became the acts of the corporation, but only in so far as they did not fall outside the powers and purposes of the corporation.

---

[81] *Glossa ordinaria* of c. 1, X, *de syndico,* I, 39, ad v. "generaliter"; Durandus, *Speculum Juris,* lib. I, partic. III, *de procuratoribus,* § 2, nos. 3-9.

[82] Gierke, *Genossenschaftsrecht,* III, 339, citing Tancredus, II, 9, 1, f. (p. 166) : "Et nota, quod, si *praelatus vel syndicus seu actor ecclesiae* petant rem ipsius ecclesiae, debent formulare libellum *nomine ecclesiae* et debent petere, sibi nomine ecclesiae ipsius rem restitui et adiudicari. Idem facere debent syndicus et actor universitatis. Nomine autem suo petere non possunt, cum nullam habeant actionem utilem vel directam."

[83] *Glossa ordinaria* of c. 1, X, *de syndico,* I, 39, ad v. "generaliter": ". . . syndicus personam sustinet universitatis vel collegii." *Glossa ordinaria* of c. 13, X, *de procuratoribus,* I, 38, ad v. "procuratoris." Cf. Innocentius IV, *Commentaria,* lib. V, tit. 39, c. 53, ad v. "consiliarios"; Hostiensis, *Summa Aurea,* lib. I, tit. 39, *de syndico,* n. 6.

[84] Gierke, *Genossenschaftsrecht,* III, 340; Hostiensis, *Summa Aurea,* lib. I, tit. 39, *de syndico,* n. 6.

In an ordinary association which had not been constituted as a moral person the members acted as natural persons and agents for one another, all their responsibilities flowing from an individual and personal source rather than from a united or moral source. But in the case of the moral person its members, though natural persons, were merged in the corporate identity. Consequently, every suit in which the moral person participated as plaintiff or as defendant, was the suit or the judicial action of the moral person as such, and not that of the members.[85] For a long time the juristic person was considered as the *domina,* but in a later period, when the distinction between the *syndicus* and *procurator* was no longer sharply drawn, the members jointly were considered in a trial to stand at least in the place of the domina.[86]

The procurators were held incompetent to take certain kinds of oaths, to effect a settlement with the creditors, or to yield to a negotiated compact or agreement. The syndic, in these cases and others, had to have recourse to the prelate, or sometimes to the community as a whole.[87]

Finally, the execution in the case had to be directed against the collegiate moral person or against its property.[88]

It was held that the principals or representatives of moral bodies were to propose the facts in a trial. This proposal of the facts was not made through the agency of advocates, unless the principals or representatives lacked prudence and discretion to such an extent that the judge allowed advocates to function for them.[89]

---

[85] Bernardus Papiensis (Faventinus Episcopus, d. 1213), *Summa Decretalium* (ed. E.A.T., Laspeyres, Ratisbonae, 1860), lib. I, tit. 29a, § 1: Hostiensis, Summa Aurea, lib. I, tit. 39, *de syndico,* n. 6.

[86] *Glossa ordinaria* of c. 7, X, *de procuratoribus,* I, 38, ad v. "de iure communi."

[87] Innocentius IV, *Commentaria,* lib. I, tit. 33, c. 1 (p. 75, col. 1, lines 7-9) : "In rebus vel negotiis universitatum sufficit requiri rectores vel idoneorum partes, et sufficit vocari praesentes; negotium quando tangit multos ut singulos, tunc singuli sunt vocandi."

[88] Durandus, *Speculum Juris,* lib. II, tit. 3, *de executione sententia,* § 3, nos. 4-5.

[89] C. 14, X, *de iudiciis,* II, 1: "Statuimus praeterea, ut principales personae non per advocatos, sed per se ipsas factum proponant, nisi forte sint adeo indiscretae, ut earum defectus de iudicis licentia per alios suppleatur."

The practice of issuing a general citation, that is, one in which simply the abbot of the monastery was cited, was acknowledged as a valid procedure. In this way notice was given to the head of the collective group of which the corporation was composed, and it was thereby made certain that the *corpus* would be represented.[90] The Roman Rota held in 1913 that the moral person, since it had a right to stand in court inasmuch as it was a true subject of rights and duties, could be cited by means of a general citation which named the administrator or the director.[91]

The competent forum was to be determined for the corporation on the basis of domicile. The corporate domicile was simply the place where its principal establishment existed.[92]

Collegiate moral persons could use the extraordinary judicial remedy of a *restitutio in integrum*.[93] This remedy was open to these persons in view of the fact that the law vindicated for them the same favorable means that it accorded to individuals who were still in their minority. The nature of the remedy, whether employed judicially or extra-judicially, was of an extraordinary kind. Its object was concerned with any matter which proved prejudicial to the moral person, once no other remedy was available for use. For example, when damage had been caused through legal prescription, the right or the thing in question was to be restored to the possession of the moral person.

---

[90] Reiffenstuel, lib. II, tit. 3, n. 57; Schmalzgrueber, lib. I, tit. 3, n. 20, ad 5.

[91] *S. Romanae Rotae Decisiones seu Sententiae* (ab anno 1909, Romae: Typis Vaticanis, 1912-), V (1913), 116-126, Decisio X, n. 8.

[92] Gregorius XVI (1831-1846) held (*Bullarii Romani Continuatio Summorum Pontificum* [19 vols., Prati, 1756-1883], XIX (1857), Parte III, tit. II, sezione 1, § 440): "Le azioni fra soci, dipendenti dai contratti di società, e quelle contro i soci, per causa della società finchè essa dura, saranno introdotte avanti il tribunale del luogo ove esiste il principale stabilimento della medesima."

[93] Cf. c. 2, X, *de in integrum restitutione,* I, 41; c. 2, X, *de consuetudine,* I, 4.

CHAPTER IV

THE EARLY HISTORY OF THE PROCEDURAL RIGHTS OF ECCLESIASTICAL CORPORATIONS IN ENGLISH COMMON LAW

ARTICLE 1. INTERRELATION OF THE COMMON LAW WITH THE CANON LAW

The fundamental notion or idea of the corporation in English law is ". . . that it is a group of individuals which is, for many purposes, treated by law as one person, and, moreover, a totally different person from the individuals who are its members."[1]

Since the time of Gratian, Canon Law has stood alongside the Civil Law as a separate—at times even a rival—body of learned jurisprudence. In the Middle Ages the universities taught, commented on and developed these two bodies of law. The term Civil Law is used here in the sense of the Roman Law. At the universities separate Faculties were maintained for the two studies, but the method employed in expounding the law was the same for both branches. The students who followed the study of Canon Law were called *decretistae* and *decretalistae*. The students who pursued the study of Civil Law were known as *legistae*. Moreover, each student received a special degree for the successful effort expended by him in his individual field.[2]

There is ample authority that Canon Law was indebted in many ways to Civil Law. Ecclesiastical procedure law had, in fact, been founded on the law of the Empire. The *Code* and the *Digest* of Justinian offered ecclesiastical legislators and lawyers a source of training in legal method and technique. Canonists incorporated into the canonical system the greater part of the Roman Law of pro-

---

[1] Jenks, *The Book of English Law* (Boston: Houghton, Mifflin Co., 1929), p. 139.

[2] Holdsworth, *A History of English Law* (3. ed., 9 vols., London: Methuen, 1923), II, 141.

cedure. Gratian was often interpreted by means of a direct appeal to Justinian's juridical thought.[3]

On the other hand, the Common Law of the Middle Ages was indebted, in many ways, to the ecclesiastical law. Canon Law during that period was a living and growing legal organism. It was adapting itself to new rules, both in the substantive and procedural law. The growing states of the then culturally progressive Europe took advantage of this advancement in jurisprudence, and from the classical texts these states evolved rules for their own guidance.[4]

During the period of the Frankish Kingdom of the Merovingians (A. D. 481-752) the Church existed under the Roman law. In that period churches were considered to be corporations or juristic persons. However, the Teutonic mind took a long time to grasp this involved or complex notion.[5] New influences later came to affect the Germanic attitude towards the corporation. For example, with the disappearance of the Roman emperors in the West and the coming of the great schism between the East and West, binding papal decretals were issued in ecclesiastical matters, and from time to time there were held general councils which legislated on matters of faith and discipline. Then too, there occurred a series of *Capitula,* convoked as the result of the alliance between the Church and the Carolingian dynasty. One can note, in this brief way, how the forces of legislative and judicial power became strengthened in both Church and State with a progressively larger share of independence acknowledged as belonging to the Church.[6]

With the Norman Conquest (1066) England was brought into contact with the continental intellectual trends. Before the invasion, except for a short space of time, England had remained adamant in

---

[3] Holdsworth, *loc. cit.;* cf. Pollock and Maitland, *A History of English Law* (2. ed., 2 vols., Cambridge: University Press. 1923), I, 95; Jenks, *Law and Politics in the Middle Ages* (New York: Holt & Co., 1898), 26-29 (hereafter cited *Law and Politics*) ; Augustine, *A Commentary on the New Code of Canon Law* (8 vols. Vol. I, 6. ed., 1931; Vol. II, 6. ed., 1936; Vol. III, 5. ed., 1938; Vol. IV, 3. ed., 1925; Vol. V, 5. ed., 1935; Vol. VI, 3. ed., 1931; Vol. VII, 3. ed., 1930; Vol. VIII, 3. ed., 1931, St. Louis: Herder & Co.), VII, 1 (hereafter cited as *A Commentary*).

[4] Holdsworth, *op. cit.,* II, 142.

[5] Pollock and Maitland, *op. cit.,* I, 469-495.

[6] Jenks, *Law and Politics,* pp. 26-29.

her attachment to her own system of jurisprudence based on the natural law. She had refused to receive Roman law, and accordingly had developed her own system.[7] But with the Norman Conquest England came under the influence of a most progressive and, it may be said, the best governed cosmopolitan people of the time. Within less than a century the first and only Englishman ever to occupy the Chair of Peter was elected Pope, Adrian IV (1154-1159).

While it is probably true that England received little from the Norman institutions themselves, she did gain a tremendous amount from her introduction to the policies and thoughts of the Europeans. Her laws received a definite shape from men who availed themselves of this legal renaissance, so to speak, brought to her shores with the Conquest. For example, the painstaking study of Gratian and the Glossators, who were acquainted to a high degree not only with Canon Law but also with Civil Law, was in due course to become as common a pursuit among Englishmen as it was among the continental Europeans. These external influences, which shaped the course of the English law, may be said to have been the most important of all such influences.[8]

English lawyers and students, during the XII century, did not neglect the study of Roman Law, although the great majority of them had to travel to Paris and Bologna for that purpose.[9] At the same time works and treatises on civil law existed in the English monastic libraries.[10] It is to certain tracts on procedure which appeared in the XII and XIII centuries on the continent that Englishmen owe one of the main sources for later works. But after the end of the thirteenth century the study of the Civil and the Canon Law did not directly influence the growth of the English law.[11]

The dual training in civil and ecclesiastical legal thought enabled the English to construct a general, logical and specific system of

---

[7] Salmond, *Jurisprudence*, p. 35.

[8] Holdsworth, *op. cit.*, II, 146.

[9] Stubbs, *Lectures on Medieval and Modern History* (3. ed., Oxford, 1900), p. 349. Cf. Haskins, *Norman Institutions* (Cambridge: Harvard University Press, 1925), p. 330.

[10] Pollock and Maitland, *op. cit.*, I, 100.

[11] Holdsworth, *op. cit.*, I, 176-177.

jurisprudence out of a rather indefinite and often conflicting mass of custom—half tribal and half feudal.[12]

ARTICLE 2. THE MEDIEVAL (1066-1485) COMMON LAW

While the canonical theories of juridical being helped the common law lawyers in England to ascertain the nature of the incorporated person, English law, in respect to the manner of creating corporate bodies and certain other factors, possessed certain native rules pertaining to these bodies.[13] With the acceptance of juridic personal entities in English law, questions began to arise concerning the powers, capacities and liabilities of the corporation. Among the rights recognized were the power to own real and personal property, the capacity to initiate a suit and to respond to a suit initiated by others, and the ability to make contracts. The responsibility for wrongs done to others was also recognized in the corporations as owners of property.[14]

England, during the period here under discussion, recognized that with reference to the friars and the religious the Pope could incorporate them in a moral unity or juridic personality.[15]

In the year 1476 it was held that "a man shall not have a writ of trespass against an abbot and convent because the convent cannot commit a trespass. . . ."[16] This decision tended to restrict the view which upheld the delictual capacity of corporations. It also had

---

[12] Holdsworth, *op. cit.,* I, 177.

[13] Holdsworth, *op. cit.,* III, 477.

[14] Holdsworth, *op. cit.,* III, 488.

[15] Brown, *Juristic Personality,* p. 38—citing Y.B. 14 Hen. VIII, f. 3 (Mich. pl. 2). The Year Books mentioned in this dissertation are law reports. Originally these reports existed only in manuscript form. They were written and many times transcribed during the period of 1283-1535. They were called "Year Books" for the reason that the cases were grouped by regnal years. But the title does not mean to imply that the reports were published annually or immediately after the year the case was decided.—Hicks, *Materials and Methods of Legal Research* (3. rev. ed., Rochester, New York · Lawyers Co-operative Company, 1942), p. 115.

[16] Holdsworth, *op. cit.,* III, 488—citing Y.B. 15 Ed. IV, Mich. pl. 2. Cf. Pollock, "Has the Common Law Received The Fiction Theory of Corporations?"—27 *The Law Quarterly Review* (London, 1885-), 219-235, esp. p. 233.

some effect in the determination of the corporate powers in other ways. But this decision, as well as others, was reached on "considerations of expediency" rather than on any "attempt to work out logical deductions drawn from the nature of the corporate personality.[17]

Just as canonical jurisprudence had indeed to some extent restricted, but by no means completely denied, the capacity of a corporation to commit delicts, so the English law also found no difficulty in holding the corporate body liable for certain kinds of wrongs. The acknowledged delictual capacity of a corporation was clearly restricted in certain directions. But in English law the idea of delictual wrong-doing was founded rather on an act which, in being legally wrong, had occasioned damage to another. The English law held the corporation liable for such wrongs when they were committed either against a person or against another corporation.[18]

In the year 1307 the Church was recognized in a case as a legal personality, and the right of *restitutio in integrum* was conceded to it.[19]

Holdsworth furnishes a series of citations from the Year Books, showing the various procedural rights of the corporation. These rights will be given a brief mention here.[20] The corporation was held liable if through its agent damage was caused to another.[21] The rule developed and became fixed that a corporation was bound to its consent only when a sealed instrument attesting it could be put in evidence.[22] But certain exceptions were permitted with reference to this rule. If a corporation had acquired certain property under a contract, it had to pay for it, and it was no defense that there was lacking a contract under seal. In certain matters of less importance a seal was not required.[23]

The rules of law on corporations were as yet meager, but it was

---

[17] Holdsworth, *op., cit.*, III, 488.

[18] Holdsworth, *op. cit.*, III, 489—citing Y.BB. 45 Ed. III, Hil. pl. 5; 46 Ed. III, Mich. pl. 7; 32 Hy. VI, Mich. pl. 13.

[19] Pollock and Maitland, *A History of English Law,* I, 484.

[20] Holdsworth, *op. cit.*, III, 484, 485, 489.

[21] Y.B. 48 Ed. III, Trin. pl. 2 per Belknap.

[22] Y.B. 22 Hy. VI, Mich. pl. 6.

[23] Y.B. 4 Hy. VII, Pasch. pl. 2.

from these decisions that later English law rules were developed. The corporations could not be outlawed;[24] it could not be excommunicated;[25] it could not be assaulted or imprisoned;[26] and could not commit treason or felony.[27] It was mentioned in one case that the canonists held that a corporation could not commit a sin or a delict.[28]

In 1476 there was an action of debt on a sealed bond against an abbot and the convent. It was pleaded that the abbot's predecessor had compelled his monks under duress to execute the deed.[29] This was held to be no plea. Brian (Chief Justice) held that the monastery as a moral person was not liable, for the simple reason that all the individual monks had acted under duress.

It was held in another case that, if an abbot, a prior, a dean or a master was suing in a trial which had opened before his election to his present office, he had to show that he had been duly elected as head of the corporate body.[30]

---

[24] 22 Ass. pl. 67; Y.BB. 45 Ed. III, Hil. pl. 5; 21 Ed. IV, pp. 13-14.

[25] Y.B. 21 Ed. IV, p. 14 per Choke.

[26] Y.B. 21 Ed. IV, pp. 13-14.

[27] Y.B. 21 Ed. IV, p. 13 per Pigot.

[28] Y.B. 15 Ed. IV, Mich. pl. 2 per Brian.

[29] Y.B. 15 Ed. IV, Mich. pl. 2. Cf. Pollock, "Has the Common Law Received the Fiction Theory of Corporations?"—27 *The Law Quarterly Review* 233.

[30] Y.B. 34 Hy. VI, Mich. pl. 6.

CANONICAL COMMENTARY

CHAPTER V

Contentious Actions by and Against the Collegiate Moral Person

Article 1. Contentious Actions in General

The official promulgation of the *Codex* was made under the Pontificate of Benedict XV in the Constitution *Providentissima Mater* of May 27, 1917, the Feast of Pentecost.[1] This Constitution decreed that the *Codex* would have the force of law from the Feast of Pentecost May 19, 1918. From this date, the *Codex Iuris Canonici* became the one authentic source of the general legislation of the Catholic Church, *unicus et authenticus fons.*[2] It is true that the material law, the substance of the law, was not changed by the Church in such a manner or to such a degree that it might be said that an entirely new period or epoch in Church discipline has been achieved. But the formal law, the wording of the legal text, as contained in the Code, is now the only source of the general ecclesiastical or canonical discipline. Therefore, the present Code, becomes the official authentic source, and the so-called "old law" becomes the historical source.

Although in the Code of Canon Law there is not to be found a definition of the juristic person, there are nevertheless various canons of the Code which deal directly with the collegiate moral person. For example, in the *Liber Secundus,* entitled *De Personis,* there are several canons devoted to the nature, constitution, rights and obligations of the collegiate body.[3] In the *Liber Tertius,* part six concerning the temporal goods of the Church applies in great

[1] Cicognani, *Canon Law* (2. rev. ed., Authorized version by J. M. O'Hara and F. Brennan, Philadelphia: The Dolphin Press, 1935), p. 423.

[2] Sacra Congregatio de Seminariis et Universitatibus Studiorum, 7 aug. 1917—*AAS,* IX (1917), 439 (hereafter cited as S.C. de Sem. et Univ. Stud.).

[3] Canons 99; 100; 101; 102; 105; 106.

part to the juristic person.[4] Again, in the *Liber Quartus,* entitled *De Processibus,* there are a number of canons which directly bear on the ecclesiastical corporation.[5] Lastly, in the *Liber Quintus,* entitled *De Delictis et Poenis,* the corporate capacity to commit a delict or crime is treated, and also the punishment to be inflicted for such delicts.[6]

The canons in the *Liber Quartus* and the *Liber Quintus* are more pertinent to this dissertation than those in the other books of the Code, and will be discussed at length in the forthcoming pages. But besides and beyond these various canons and parts of the Code of Canon Law which deal directly in whole or in part with the collegiate moral person in regard to its rights and duties, there are numerous other canons of the Code which also have a legal application to these persons, at least indirectly.[7]

Of these canons of the Code of Canon Law which have a legal significance for the collegiate moral person because of indirect reference the writer will have more to say in the succeeding pages. It will suffice that one example of this category be set forth at this time. Since, for example, all moral ecclesiastical persons, in general, and the collegiate moral person, in particular, are assimilated to minors[8] and therefore enjoy the rights and privileges of minors, there are many canons of the Code which have application to the collegiate moral person because of this provision of law. This assimilation of corporate entities to minors is based on the reason that the moral body is a being whose purely legal status prevents it from acting for itself; its management is under the control of its administrators just as the management of the property of the minor stands under the control of his parents or guardians. As in the case of the minor, it is possible that it may suffer irreparable or serious damage through the negligence of its administrators, for which an action of *restitutio in integrum* would arise.[9]

---

[4] Canons 1499-1551 inclusive.

[5] Canons 1552; 1557; 1560; 1649; 1653.

[6] Canons 2255; 2274; 2285; 2291.

[7] Canon 1553; 1554; 1561 et cetera.

[8] Canon 100, § 3.

[9] Canon 1687, § 1; cf. canons 1682; 1737; Coronata, *Institutiones,* I, n. 139; Blat, *Commentarium,* lib. II, pars I, n. 31.

Upon a consideration in general perspective of the various parts and canons of the Code of Canon Law which concern the collegiate moral person, a brief statement of the nature and scope of the term "contentious action" is in order.

The *Liber Quartus* of the Code presents the legislation on processes. The term "process" is of the generic kind. It denotes a series of acts which the law prescribes for the judicial or extrajudicial treatment of questions and the execution of matters by public authority. The *iudicium* or the trial is defined as the legitimate discussion and definition of a controverted matter which the Church has the right to judge, before a duly constituted ecclesiastical tribunal. A contentious trial has for its object the vindication or attainment of the rights of physical or moral persons, or the declaration of juridical facts concerning such persons.[10]

In the *Liber Quintus,* the expression *"forum contentiosum"* in canon 2237, § 1, 1°, denotes a judicial forum without distinction, and hence comprises courts sitting for both contentious and criminal trials.[11] Likewise, *"actio poenalis"* in canons 2210, § 1, 1°, and 2240 denotes a criminal action, and the *"actio civilis"* in canon 2210, § 1, 2°, and § 2, clearly signifies a contentious trial. But, consistently the codifiers of the Code in the *Liber Quartus* have substituted the term "contentious" for "civil," thus deviating from the pre-Code terminology of "civil" and "criminal."[12]

Canon 1552, § 2, distinguishes between two classes of procedure. One class is the contentious trial and the other is the criminal trial. From the point of view of the object of the trial the Code defines a contentious trial as the prosecution or vindication of the rights of physical or of moral persons, or the declaration of the juridical facts concerning such persons.[13] The criminal case, as defined by

---

[10] Canon 1552. Cf. Król, *The Defendant in Contentious Trials,* The Catholic University of America Canon Law Studies, n. 146 (Washington, D. C.: The Catholic University of America Press, 1942), p. 2.

[11] Wernz-Vidal, *Ius Canonicum,* VII, n. 214; Coronata, *Institutiones,* IV, n. 1737; Roberti, *De Delictis et Poenis* (1 vol. in 2, Romae: Apud Aedes Facultatis Iuridicae ad S. Apollinaris, 1930-1938), n. 270 (hereafter cited *De Delictis*).

[12] Roberti, *De Processibus,* 1 (2. ed., Romae: Apud Custodiam Librariam Pontificii Instituti Utriusque Iuris, 1941), n. 57.

[13] Canon 1552, § 2, 1°.

the Code in canon 1552, § 2, 2°, is concerned with a trial of offenses to the end that a penalty may be declared or inflicted. The contentious trial is concerned with the private good; the criminal with the public good.[14] Let it be supposed, for example, that a duly constituted ecclesiastical corporation has a cause of action because of some sustained wrong or injury in which it seeks satisfaction commensurate with the damage sustained. The wrong or injury may affect the corporation alone, i.e., it may affect solely a private interest. Under canon 1534, which permits personal or real actions because of unlawful alienation of property, the action is of a private nature and touches only private persons. If an ecclesiastical corporation were involved in this type of suit, the suit would be, because of the private nature of the corporation, a contentious one under the Code. Let it now be supposed that the corporate entity brought suit not for its own private interests, but in order to protect the welfare of the community or of the public order in general. This type of action would be a criminal one in nature, seeking the vindication or restoration of the public order, and not simply that of private interests. In this latter type of case the corporation would be the accuser, and the Church, as guardian of the public order, would be the prosecutor through its public officer.

Controverted rights are the material object of a trial; judicial actions are the formal object.[15] Canon 1667 declares that every right can be enforced not only by means of an action in court, unless the contrary is expressly stated, but also by means of an exception, which is always available and is of its own nature perpetual.

The judicial action in contentious cases is of two classes: either a proprietary suit (*actio petitoria*), or a possessory suit (*actio possessoria*). The former consists in the vindication or prosecution of one's right under the law. The latter type is an action to obtain the possession of a *res,* or a quasi-possession, if there be question of obtaining the free exercise of one's rights.[16]

---

[14] Regatillo, *Institutiones*, II, n. 329, p. 157; Vermeersch-Creusen, *Epitome,* III, n. 4, p. 3.

[15] Lega-Bartoccetti, *Commentarius in Iudicia Ecclesiastica iuxta Codicem Iuris Canonici* (3 vols., Romae; Anonima Libraria Cattolica Italiana, 1938-1941), I, 3 (hereafter cited *Commentarius*).

[16] Canon 1668.

The ecclesiastical corporation, for example, may be a plaintiff in a proprietary suit which bases its claim to a thing or to a right inasmuch as the law gives it title thereto;[17] it may also be a plaintiff in a possessory action which claims the possession of a corporeal thing, or a quasi-possession of an incorporeal thing.[18] The declaration of a juridical fact, such as the status of persons arising from the administration of the sacraments, for example, of matrimony and of Holy Orders, may be obtained according to Lega (1860-1935)-Bartoccetti[19] in a proprietary suit. Wernz (1842-1914)-Vidal (1867-1938),[20] on the other hand, were of the opinion that the declaration of juridical facts is not properly sought directly in such an action. The present writer is of the opinion that the term *actio petitoria* is broad enough in its scope to include petitions seeking a declaration of juridical facts.

In any event, this particular type of contentious action would not be open to the ecclesiastical corporation, since it is concerned rather with the issue as directly bearing on the common good in its "transcendental phase," i.e., the relation of the individual to God, or the ultimate common good of man.[21] The ecclesiastical corporation is certainly not capable of receiving the sacraments.

However, since it is easily supposed that the proprietary action could be concerned with a declaration of status not directly associable with the administration of the sacraments such as a declaration relative to the question of legitimate birth,[22] the writer believes that such an action might be open to the ecclesiastical corporation with a view to establishing its legal status as a corporation under the ecclesiastical law. But the authors consulted fail to mention this possibility, although a declaration of a juridical fact may be

---

[17] Noval, *De Iudiciis*, n. 303; Lega-Bartoccetti, *Commentarius*, I, 367; Coronata, *Institutiones*, III, n. 1196.

[18] Wernz-Vidal, *Ius Canonicum*, VI, n. 249; Noval, *loc. cit.*; Augustine, *A Commentary*, VII, 120-121. Canon 1668, § 2 by implication defines quasi possession as referable to rights properly possessed by one as incorporeal things, for example, the right of election.

[19] *Commentarius*, I, p. 3, n. 5.

[20] *Ius Canonicum, loc. cit.*

[21] Król, *The Defendant in Contentious Trials*, p. 3.

[22] Lega-Bartoccetti, *op. cit.*, I, 3, n. 5.

made by a court under canon 1552, § 2, 1°.[23] There seems to be no question that the corporation could establish its legal status in both the *actio petitoria* and the *actio possessoria,* at least indirectly.

The following actions are classified as proprietary:[24] actions of sequestration of goods and the injunction of the exercise of rights; actions to stop new enterprises and to obtain security against danger to one's property; actions arising from the nullity of acts; and, finally, actions for rescissions and *restitutio in integrum.*

The various kinds of possessory actions are exemplified in the following: the *actio rei adipiscendae,* by which a person claims under some color of title the right of obtaining a thing which he is not now possessed of:[25] the *actio retinendae possessionis,* by which a person claims the right of retaining the thing which he now is possessed of;[26] and, finally, the *actio recuperandae possessionis,* by which a person claims the right of recovering the thing which he was earlier dispossessed of.[27]

---

[23] *American Law:* The idea of a declaratory judgment is of comparatively recent development. State ex rel. La Follette v. Dammann, 220 Wisc. 17, 264 N.W. 627. *A Uniform Declaratory Judgments Act* has been adopted in many states, although in some cases with slight modification, that is, in Alabama, Arizona, Colorado, Idaho, Indiana, Minnesota, Missouri, Montana, Nebraska, Nevada, New Jersey, North Carolina, North Dakota, Ohio, Oregon, Pennsylvania, South Dakota, Tennessee, Utah, Vermont, Washington, Wisconsin and Wyoming.

The distinctive characteristic of a declaratory judgment is that it is merely affirmatory, and not coercive. No executory process follows as of course. Cf. Carmody, *A Treatise on New York Practice* (rev. by Carr, New York: Clark Boardman Co., Ltd., 1931), § 485. Declaratory judgments have been made concerning various matters in relation to private corporations: (e.g., Sullivan & Sons Mfg. Co. v. Ideal Bldg. & Loan Assoc., 313 Pa. 407) such as the validity and the construction of their charters or articles of association (Cf. 12 A.L.R. 87; 19 A.L.R. 1135; 68 A.L.R. 130; 87 A.L.R. 1236), the existence of the corporation, the classification to which it belongs, and the rights, powers and obligations attaching to it (Bartlett v. Lily Dale Assembly, 139 Misc. 338, 249 N. Y. Supp. 482).

[24] Cf. Beste, *Introductio in Codicem* (2. ed., Collegeville, Minn.: St. John's Abbey Press, 1944), can. 1668 (hereafter cited as *Introductio*).

[25] Canon 1693.

[26] Canons 1695-1697.

[27] Canon 1698.

There also arises from the commission of an offense a contentious action for the reparation of losses incurred if such were sustained.[28] This contentious action is to be conducted in accordance with canons 1552-1959.[29] Therefore, the tort action may be either proprietary or possessory in nature, depending on the nature of the case. The same judge who hears the criminal action can at the instance of the injured party try and decide the contentious action connected therewith.[30]

ARTICLE 2. JURIDIC CAPACITY

Since this chapter treats of the collegiate moral person in the contentious trials, there arises the question whether the juristic person in itself—since it is a legal person, though it is unlike in nature to that of the physical person—has the juridical capacity to sue and to be sued. In short, can the collegiate moral person be a plaintiff or a defendant in contentious trials before a duly constituted ecclesiastical court or tribunal? In a subsequent chapter a discussion of the legal person's capacity to be a party defendant in a criminal trial before a Church court or tribunal will be set forth.

The status of a moral person is its position as a distinct personality, involving its legal capacity to exercise certain rights and to be subject to certain obligations or duties. The Code, however, does not determine every general right of the various species of moral persons. Generally it may be affirmed that all moral persons have the rights of acquiring temporal goods and of administering them,[31] of acquiring privileges and indults,[32] of enjoying the prerogatives consequent on the factor of precedence,[33] of honoring the fulfillment of vows previously taken, of abiding by their previously established and approved constitutions and rules,[34] and,

[28] Canon 2210, § 1, 2°. This type of contentious trial is commonly known as the tort action.

[29] Canon 2210, § 2.

[30] Canon 2210, § 2.

[31] Canon 1495, § 2.

[32] Canon 4.

[33] Canon 106.

[34] Canon 1253.

finally, of acting as party convening (plaintiff) and party convened (defendant) in trials.[35]

The basis for the proposition that the collegiate moral person may sue and be sued is indicated expressly in canons 100, § 3, 1552, § 2, 1°, 1649 and 1653. In the canonical use of the term "express" the meaning of "implied" as well as the meaning of "explicit" is included as a species under its genus. Canon 100, § 3, states that the legal person, whether collegiate or non-collegiate, is regarded as equivalent to minors. It can be inferred logically that, since the minor has the right to sue and to be sued, or to be a party litigant in an ecclesiastical trial, so likewise the corporate body which is like the minor in the eyes of the law enjoys this right.

Canon 1552, § 2, 1°, states that the subject matter of canonical trials consists in the prosecution or vindication of the rights of physical or of moral persons, or in the declaration of the juridical facts concerning such persons. Legally considered, this canon is one which declares the subject matter of judicial jurisdiction. It has not for its main purpose the stating of the substantive right of the collegiate moral person to stand in court. Rather, the canon deals with a jurisdictional issue regarding the distinction between judicial actions. But Coronata rightly cites canon 1552, § 2, 1° to support the proposition that the moral person may sue and be sued.[36]

---

[35] Canons 1552, § 2, 1°; 1649, 1653. *American Law:* All corporations of whatever kind are circumscribed and controlled by their charters or acts of incorporation, which to them are the laws of their being, which they can neither dispense with nor alter. Subject, however, to such limitations as these, or such as may be prescribed by the general statutes or constitutional law, every corporation aggregate has, by virtue of incorporation and incidental thereto, the power to sue and be sued—Bouvier, *Dictionary,* I, 684, ad v. "Corporation"; cf. Baltimore & P. R. Co. v. Fifth Baptist Church, 137 U. S. 568, 34 L. Ed. 784, 11 Sup. Ct. 185.

The right to sue and to be sued is expressed in the various state constitutions and statutory enactments, with the exception of the State of New York, where the right is considered as an implied one of incorporation (cf. *Corporation Manual,* New York: United States Corporation Company, 1946). The power of a corporation to sue includes the power to take every step that an individual may take to reach a final judgment (cf. Alexander Canal Company v. Swann, 5 How. 83, 12 L. Ed. 60).

[36] *Institutiones,* I, n. 139.

On the other hand, canon 1649 states that the collegiate and the non-collegiate moral persons are to be represented in court by the rector or the administrator, except in special cases mentioned in canon 1653. But canons 1649 and 1653 in fact declare also the procedural capacity of the corporate body, or the manner in which the collegiate moral person is to act either as party plaintiff or party defendant in a trial. Canon 1649 was not incorporated in the Code as a positive declaration that the juristic person has the right to sue and to be sued. In any event, it is nevertheless most certainly clear from the canons cited that the ecclesiastical corporation has the right to sue others and to defend itself against others in order to prosecute and vindicate its rights in a canonical trial.

The various commentators on the Code of Canon Law are unanimous in their views that the juristic person may be a party plaintiff or a party defendant.[37] The Code attributes other rights to special moral persons, but not to all, such as, for example, the right to legislate and to enact statutory laws for itself.[38] These rights are separate and distinct from the rights of the members who constitute the corporate legal body.[39]

The ecclesiastical corporation, then, is able to have all the rights and obligations which a physical person can have, except such as intrinsically or in consequence of the positive law are proper to

---

[37] Chelodi, *Ius Canonicum de Personis* (3. ed., curavit P. Ciprotti, Trento: Liberia Moderna Editrice, 1942), n. 99; Lega-Bartoccetti, *Commentarius,* I, p. 307, n. 7; Coronata, *Institutiones,* I, n. 139 (VI); Roberti, *De Processibus,* I, p. 544, n. 198, II; Wernz-Vidal, *Ius Canonicum,* II, n. 32; Cappello, *Summa,* p. 40; Regatillo, *Institutiones,* I, n. 206; Gillet, *La Personalité Juridique,* p. 120; Brown, *Juristic Personality,* p. 98; Blat, *Commentarium,* lib. II, pars I, n. 31; Augustine, *A Commentary,* VII, 98 ff.

[38] Canons 410; 689; 697.

[39] "Itaque ex dictis liquet, 1° personam moralem iura diversa et omnino distincta habere a iuribus *singulorum* membrorum; 2° huiusmodi iura subsistere *independenter* ab eorum nutu et assensu; 3° ipsam *exsistentiam* personae moralis eiusque *conversationem* et *operationem* prorsus *independentem* esse a *singulorum;* arbitrio; 4° his cessantibus, *non ideo cessare* personem moralem, quae nihilominus manet, suumque statum iuridicum integrum atque incolumem servat."—Cappello, *Summa,* n. 39, 3, p. 41.

physical persons alone, e.g., the right to contract marriage, or the right to renounce a privilege which has been established by law.[40]

ARTICLE 3. JURISDICTION CONCERNING JURISTIC PERSONS

The judicial power of the Church is the right in a particular case to declare authentically the true meaning of the law, and to judge whether the acts of the subjects of the Church in such a particular case are or are not in conformity with the law.[41] This power flows naturally from the right to enact laws. The basis of the judicial power rests upon the jurisdiction of the person or persons exercising that power. The term jurisdiction (*ius dicere*) in present canonical procedural law comprises the power of the presiding judicial officer of the ecclesiastical tribunal to hear and determine a suit. Whether the court is composed of one or of more judges, it still acts as one. The test of jurisdiction is whether the court has the right to hear and decide a controversy. Canon Law derived the notion of jurisdiction from the Roman Law and from the tradition of the Middle Ages.[42] In the strict sense of the term, the exercise of judicial jurisdiction consists in the function of judging in trials; of defining and examining the controverted issue.[43] Its foundation is rooted in the determining of issues or of counts (*dubia*);[44] its object is to solve a controversy[45] and to terminate a trial by means of a definitive sentence or solution.[46]

Since there are two specifically distinct perfect societies, the Church and the State, there are two supreme authorities, lay and ecclesiastical, and hence two jurisdictions or judicial powers. The limits between the sphere of each power or jurisdiction are defined

---

[40] Canon 72, § 4. Coronata, *Institutiones,* I, n. 139. A moral person, such as a religious order or a collegiate chapter, can in law enjoy the juridical status of a canonical pastor to whom title to a parish may be given along with the care of souls to be exercised under the authority of the local ordinary. Cf. canon 451, § 1.

[41] Cf. canon 17, § 3.

[42] Roberti, *De Processibus,* I, n. 46.

[43] Canons 1553, § 1; 1961; 1970.

[44] Canons 1728; 1729, §§ 1, 2.

[45] Canons 1552, § 2; 1579, §§ 1, 3; 1632; 1633; 1706; 1727; 1806.

[46] Canon 1873, § 1, 3°; cf. canon 1569, § 2.

by the nature of the suits and by the status of the persons in litigation. But there can be cases which concern both powers or jurisdictions, inasmuch as the cases are of a mixed nature. The Code has determined cases over which the Church has jurisdiction by reason of a proper and exclusive right. Such cases are those relating to spiritual matters or to temporal matters inseparably annexed to the spiritual;[47] violations of ecclesiastical laws; all other actions in which sin is involved insofar as an official declaration of guilt and an authoritative infliction of canonical penalties are concerned; and all contentious and criminal cases of persons who enjoy the privilege of the ecclesiastical forum, as defined by canons 120, 614, 680.[48]

Therefore, there is no difficulty in recognizing the Church's jurisdiction under its judicial power to hear and decide cases of collegiate moral persons, whether as plaintiffs or as defendants, when the subject matter is within the sphere of action reserved solely to the Church, or when it is of a mixed nature as set forth in canon 1553. Nor can there be any dispute in these types of cases about the juridical right of the moral person, duly constituted by the Church, to submit its case to her jurisdiction for judicial determination. On the other hand, there does arise the particularly interesting jurisdictional question whether the corporate person when duly constituted by the Church, enjoys the right of the *privilegium fori.*

A. *The Privilege of the Forum*

The privilege of the forum signifies that clerics as defendants, in cases both contentious and criminal, have the vindicated right to be judged by an ecclesiastical, and not by a lay, court, unless provisions to the contrary exist in certain places.[49] Purely ecclesiastical

[47] These temporal matters, although they may be such in a purely ontological sense, are nevertheless, through the particular teleological character which attaches to them, intimately connected with the spiritual, and hence fall under the exclusive jurisdiction of the Church. Types of such temporal matters inseparably annexed to the spiritual are: ecclesiastical burial, church revenues, legitimacy of children, etc. Cf. Augustine, *A Commentary,* VII, 5.

[48] Canon 1553.

[49] Canons 120; 1553, § 1, 3°.

cases are not dealt with here, for in them clerics and laymen are alike subject to ecclesiastical authority alone.[50] Here are considered only those temporal cases, such as those arising from wills, inheritances and patrimony, which, because of their connection with ecclesiastical persons who are held to be sacred, are withdrawn as subject-matter from the competence of the secular tribunal.

The task immediately at hand is to ascertain whether the ecclesiastical corporate person enjoys the privilege of the forum as it is strictly understood. Although canonists have examined to a considerable extent the limits of the *privilegium fori* concerning physical persons, its application to juristic persons has not been fully treated or discussed.[51]

1. *Pre-Code Law.* The privilege of the forum was generally enjoyed by the ecclesiastical collegiate moral person, although many times an accurate distinction between the person representing and the corporate person or body represented was lacking.[52]

The Council of Trent (1545-1563) recalled to secular powers their obligation to defend the clergy and the property of the Church against all who attacked their liberty, jurisdiction and immunity, and added another important phrase which, while concerned with the juridical origin of immunity, vindicated generally the immunity of the Church and of ecclesiastical persons.[53]

Besides, whenever the Church left the exercise of judging to the secular powers, it did so in such a manner that there was no doubt

---

[50] Canon 1553, § 1.

[51] Roberti, *De Processibus,* I, n. 54, p. 145; Ciprotti, "De Privilegio Fori quoad Personas Iuridicas"—*Antonianum* (Romae, 1926-), XII (1937), 165-170, and especially p. 170 (hereafter cited as "De Privilegio Fori").

[52] Cf. Ciprotti, "De Privilegio Fori," *Antonianum,* XII (1937), 165, citing Bonacina, *De Censuris Ecclesiasticis in Particulari,* disp. I, q. 16, punct. 5, n. 4. Ciprotti represents Bonacina as one "qui collegium ecclesiasticum vel laicumcenset, prout maior pars membrorum sunt ecclesiastici vel laici." Ciprotti thereupon remarks: ". . . neque ceterum ipse unus ita sentit, neque primus hanc invexit doctrinam." Cf. also Paulus V, bulla *Coena Domini,* 1610—*Bullarum Diplomatum et Privilegiorum Sanctorum Pontificum Taurinensis Editio,* 24 vols. et Appendix, Augustae Taurinorum, 1857-1872), XV, n. 15. In this Papal Bull penalties were established against violators of the privileged forum.

[53] Cf. Sess. XXV, *de ref.,* c. 20.

that the Church, in its own right, could alone concede such power.[54]

The canonists of the pre-Code times incidentally showed that the moral person enjoyed the privilege of the forum. So, for example, they were of the opinion that hospices erected under the authority of the bishop were privileged.[55] Confraternities, likewise, enjoyed the privilege of the forum.[56]

Old decrees emanating from the Sacred Congregation of Ecclesiastical Immunity, which had been established by Pope Urban VIII (1623-1644) on June 22, 1626, to protect and defend ecclesiastical immunity and jurisdiction indicate that the moral person had the right to enjoy the privileged forum under the former law.[57]

---

[54] *Raccolta di Concordati su Materie Ecclesiastiche tra la Santa Sede e le Autorità Civili* (ed. A. Mercati, Roma: Tipografia Poliglotta Vaticana, 1919): *Concordato fra Pio IX e la Republica di Guatemala,* October 7th, 1852, pp. 816-817, Art. 15: "Temporum ratione habita, Sanctitas Sua consentit, ut causae civiles Clericorum ad laicos judices deferantur, sive personales sint, sive reales, quae scilicet possessiones, atque alia temporalia Clericorum, Ecclesiarum, Beneficiorum, aliarumque Ecclesiasticarum fundationum jura respiciant. Si vero contigerit, ut inter Ecclesiasticos Viros habeantur quaestiones, illas Episcopi veluti arbitri dirimere aut conciliare poterunt; ita ut quoties hujusmodi experimentum omittatur, et desit legale documentum, ex quo constet experimentum idem absque ullo effectu fuisse peractum, nullum Status tribunal poterit actorum petitiones admittere, et ad illarum cognitionem procedere." Cf. also in the *Raccolta: Concordato colla Republica di Colombia,* July 20th, 1892, pp. 1061-1068, Art. 1; *Concordato fra Pio IX e la Republica di Honduras,* July 9th, 1861, pp. 936, 948, n. 14; *Concordato fra Pio IX e la Republica di Nicaragua,* November 2nd, 1861, pp. 948-959, Art. 13; *Concordato fra Pio e la Republica di S. Salvador,* April 22nd, 1862, pp. 960-970, Art. 14; *Nova versione del concordato della Republica dell'Equatore,* May 2nd, 1881, pp. 1001, 1013, Art. VIII.

[55] Pirhing, lib. II, tit. II, sect. III, n. 97; Fagnanus, *Commentaria in Quinque Libros Decretalium* (4 vols., Romae, 1661), lib. II, tit. II, sect. 4, n. 71 (hereafter cited Fagnanus); Barbosa, *Pastoralis Sollicitudinis sive de Officio et Potestate Episcopi Tripartita Descriptio* (Lugduni, 1656), Pars Tertia, Alleg. 75, nn. 21, 22.

[56] Ferraris, *Prompta Bibliotheca Canonica, Iuridica, Moralis, Theologica, nec non Ascetica, Polemica, Rubricistica* Historica (9 vols., Romae, 1885-1899), ad v. "Forum" n. 57 (hereafter cited as *Bibliotheca*).

[57] This Congregation issued many decrees, although no official collection of its acts was ever compiled. Cf. Downs, *The Concept of Clerical Immunity,* The Catholic University of America Canon Law Studies, n. 126 (Washington, D. C.: The Catholic University of America Press, 1941), p. 31. Pope

There is therefore, in conclusion, some very important evidence that in pre-Code legislation the moral person was given the right to enjoy the privilege of the forum.

2. *Code Legislation.* The Code is silent on the extension of the privilege of the forum to corporate persons. Whenever it treats of the *privilegium fori* it is in reference to physical persons only.[58] It is not reasonable to suppose that certain canons, such as canons 1557, § 2, and 1579, §§ 2, 3, concern themselves with the privilege of the forum, in the strict sense, in regard to the ecclesiastical corporation. Such canons as these refer rather to the exclusive jurisdiction within the Church's jurisdictional sphere of action. In other words, these canons do not indicate an exclusive jurisdiction as against even the jurisdiction of a secular court.

For example, canon 1557, § 2, states that the tribunals of the Apostolic See have the exclusive right to judge cases in which dioceses and other moral persons have no superior intermediate to the Roman Pontiff. If canon 1557, § 2, is of such a nature that it excludes the jurisdiction of secular courts as to the subject-matter mentioned therein, it must follow that those who hold the highest governmental rank in a nation, their sons and daughters, and those who have the right of succession to these places, are thereby precluded from having resort to non-ecclesiastical courts without first having obtained special permission. It is unreasonable to suppose that by canon 1557, § 1, the legislator desired to preclude laymen from having resort to a civil court for the prosecution and vindication of their rights.[59]

Again, it is true that canon 1579, §§ 2, 3, sets forth the competent court of first instance for certain specified moral persons. But in paragraph one of canon 1579 the court of first instance is declared for cases of exempt religious. If in paragraphs two and three this cited canon refers to a privileged forum for moral persons, in the

---

Pius X (1903-1914) in his reorganization of the Roman Curia in 1908 suppressed this Congregation. Ferraris (*Bibliotheca,* ad v. "Confraternitas," Art. IV) gives a brief summary of the text of some of the decrees of the Sacred Congregation of Ecclesiastical Immunity in the 17th century.

[58] Roberti, *De Processibus,* I, n. 54; Ciprotti, "De Privilegio Fori," *Antonianum,* XII (1937), 165; cf. canons 120; 614; 680; 2198; 1553, § 1, 3°.

[59] However, canon 1556 (cf. canon 100, § 1) is an exception and does exclude the jurisdiction of secular courts.—Coronata, *Institutiones,* III, n. 1095.

sense here being discussed, then it must also refer to a privileged forum for the exempt religious mentioned in paragraph one. This, too, is an unreasonable conclusion in view of canon 614, which beyond doubt alone establishes basically the privilege of the forum for religious: therefore, it is to be rightly concluded that the Code is silent on the extension of the privileged forum for corporate persons.

The writer has found only three authors.[60] who treat of the privilege of the forum for corporate bodies in the Church under the Code and they maintain that the privilege is now enjoyed by these juridical beings. Of these authors, Roberti and Ciprotti come to the same conclusion but for different reasons, which will be discussed presently. But both these authors maintain that the Code is silent on the extension of the privilege of the forum for moral persons.

Primarily because of the Code's silence on this matter, the present writer is of the opinion that, although the corporate person enjoyed the *privilegium fori* under the former law, the privilege does not exist for the juridical being under the Code legislation. The Code abolished this privilege for these persons by canon 6, n. 6 which holds that all disciplinary laws which were in force before the enactment of the Code, but are now neither explicitly nor implicitly contained in the Code, have lost all force of law. In other words, laws which were omitted in the Code are abrogated. The primary purpose of the legislator in canon 6, n. 6 was to discard the useless and the obsolete laws. This was done simply by way of omission.[61] Silence means that the Code does not expressly or implicitly mention the privilege for the juridical entities. This is exactly the situation intended to be covered by canon 6, n. 6. There-

---

[60] Roberti, *De Processibus,* I, n. 54, p. 145; Ciprotti, "De Privilegio Fori," Antonianum, XII (1937), 165-170; Cocchi, *Commentarium in Codicem Iuris Canonici* (8 vols. in 5, 1920-1930, Vol. VII, *De Processibus,* 3. ed., 1940, Taurinorum Augustae: Marietti), VII, 6. This last named author makes a declaration of his belief without stating reasons.

[61] Cf. Neuberger, *Canon 6,* The Catholic University of America Canon Law Studies, n. 44 (Washington, D. C.: The Catholic University of America, 1927), p. 60.

fore, the privilege of the forum, although it existed before the Code for corporate bodies, is no longer in force as law.[62]

There is another canon which might be briefly considered here. Ciprotti holds that canon 20 can be applied in the matter under discussion with the result that the privilege of the forum can be enjoyed by the corporate person under the Code.[63] Canon 20 states in part that if a general or a particular law contains no definite prescription concerning a matter . . . the rule for deciding such a matter must be taken from laws given in similar instances, from the general principles of Canon Law based on equity, *et cetera.* Clearly this cited canon can not be applied to set up a law for the canon speaks of a case or particular matter (*de re*) and not a norm of law for all cases of a similar nature. If canon 20 could be used to establish the privilege for moral persons, granting that an analogy or similarity exists between the corporate person and those enjoying the privilege of the forum under the Code, it would first have to be admitted that canon 20 could establish a law which was abrogated by canon 6, n. 6. This certainly was not intended to be the law by the legislator. Canon 20, therefore, applies only in a particular case and can not be employed to grant an extension of the *privilegium fori* by way of law to moral persons perforce of analogy.

Roberti maintains that the corporate person enjoys the privilege of the forum under the present legislation of the Code. This opinion introduces into the question a distinction based on the physical persons of which the moral person is composed, and analogous to the distinction between lay and ecclesiastical natural persons. It maintains that the natural persons in the Church are divided into

---

[62] Ciprotti ("De Privilegio Fori," *Antonianum,* XII, 165) maintains that canon 6, nn. 2, 4 is to be used in determining whether the privilege exists for the moral being under the Code. But a comparison of the old legislation and the new clearly indicates that there is an omission of matter in the new law. Even Roberti (*De Processibus,* I, n. 54, p. 146) maintains that there has been a tendency on the part of the Church to restrict the extension of this privilege, although he does hold that the moral person enjoys the privilege under the Code for other reasons. Canon 6, n. 4 can not be used because in reading the present law concerning the privilege of the forum no doubt exists as to the persons intended by the legislator to enjoy the privilege.

[63] Ciprotti, "De Privilegio Fori," *Antonianum,* XII (1937), 165.

ecclesiastical and lay. A like distinction is urged for the moral persons in the Church. For example, they should be divided into ecclesiastical and lay depending on the class of physical persons, in the case of collegiate bodies, or on the nature of the fund and its physical administrators, in the case of non-collegiate moral bodies. The privilege of the forum would then be extended to those moral persons which are composed or made up of members who themselves enjoy the privilege, for example, a religious order or a cathedral chapter, in the case of the collegiate moral person, while in the case of the non-collegiate person the privilege would be extended if the goods or the persons themselves are privileged, for example, a diocese.[64]

Roberti proposes that, while juridical persons have always been subjects of rights independent of physical persons, it is nevertheless true that the distinction is a mere fiction and hence exists rather as a mental abstraction or concept. Substantially, he argues, only physical persons have existence. With the aid of the abstraction that is invoked, their plurality is reduced to a unity, which principle obtains whether there be question of collegiate or of non-collegiate moral personalities.[65]

Roberti, however, readily admits that if the physical persons of whom the moral person is composed act in reality as distinct subjects, then all and each individually should acquire rights and obligations, be sued severally and cited individually. He further admits that under the law the juristic person is in fact the possessor of rights and obligations; that it can sue and be sued, and that these juridical effects flow from the moral person itself as existing separately from the persons of whom it is composed. And yet Roberti holds that the personification in law is merely fictional, conceptual or figurative, and that since the juristic person is composed of physical persons who are bound by the ends for which the group was founded, their personal status—privileged or non-privileged —should determine whether or not in the final analysis the moral person enjoys the privilege of the forum.[66]

---

[64] Roberti, *De Processibus,* I, 148.

[65] Roberti, *op. cit.,* I, 149. Roberti attributes the term "fiction" to Innocent IV (Sinibaldus Fliscus ✠ 1254).

[66] Roberti, *ibidem.*

The writer is of the opinion that whatever metaphysical basis may be the root of the juridical personality, nevertheless, these bodies have a distinct legal personality separate from that of the members, of whom as individuals they are composed.[67] If the rights of the moral person are separate and distinct from the members, there does not seem to be justifiable reasons in law for attributing the individual rights or privileges of the individuals to the corporate body. Therefore, because the members enjoy the privileged forum is no justification in law for the corporate body to possess the same privilege.[68]

---

[67] Canons 99-106.

[68] Cf. for the metaphysical concept underlying the ecclesiastical corporation —Brown, *Juristic Personality,* pp. 52-60; Hohenlohe, *Papstrecht und weltliches Recht* (München, 1925), p. 33; Dernburg, *System des römischen Rechts* (2 vols., Berlin, 1912), I, 96. *American Law*: The writer's present purpose is not to discuss the divers theories of the corporate concept in the Common Law sphere or to indulge in the tempting discussion—more metaphysical than legal—of the true nature and legal status of the corporate concept. However, several sources will be indicated here for the reader's benefit, should study along this line be undertaken. The following suggestion was made not so long ago by a rather brilliant writer: "that the corporate entity is not imaginary or fictitious but quite real, whereas the corporate personality is a true fiction whose origin is to be found in the psychological tendency towards personification. (Machen, "Corporate Personality"—24 *Harvard Law Review* 253-267, esp. p. 347.)

It would be a very difficult task to find two common law authorities in total accord as to the exact nature of the legal concept of the corporate entity and corporate personality. Civil corporations have, in the course of time, been regarded as "artificial personalities" (Dartmouth College v. Woodward, 4 Wheat. 518, 636; cf. Blackstone, *Commentaries on the Law,* I, 467-468), as "associations of individuals" (Hightower v. Thornton, 8 Ga. 486, 492; cf. Morawetz, *A Treatise on the Law of Private Corporations* [2. ed., Boston: Brown, Little, Brown, 1886], Preface) and as merely "the sum of legal relations" subsisting in respect to the corporate undertaking (Taylor, *A Treatise on the Law of Private Corporations* [Philadelphia: 1884], §§ 36, 51).

They have also been regarded as actual persons and dealt with in an anthropomorphic manner (Gierke, "Juristische Person"—*Rechtslexikon* by Holtzendorff [Leipzig: 1875], n. 943, pp. 844-849). Cf. also Canfield-Wormser, *Cases on Private Corporations* (2. ed., Indianapolis: The Bobbs-Merrill Company, 1925), pp. 1-115; Carter, *The Nature of the Corporation as a Legal Entity* (Baltimore: M. Curlander, 1919), pp. 1; 5; 114; 124; Anderson, *Limitations of the Corporate Entity,* nn. 30-36; Wormser, *Disregard of the*

There is ample evidence in the Code[69] that there are two kinds of ecclesiastical corporations, depending on the status of the members of whom they are composed, namely, religious or lay.[70] But these two classes of corporations are not so distinguished that in the Code the Church legislated a different rule of law concerning them separately, as to their creation, supervision, control and suppression. In that regard the Church makes no distinction, but treats the corporation, whether religious or lay in membership, in the same way. For example, the only division of the moral person which the Code explicitly mentions is the structural one, according to which the moral person is divided into the collegiate and non-collegiate.[71] Therefore, since the rights of the moral person whether lay or

---

Corporate Fiction and Allied Corporation Problems, see Index under "Nature of Corporation"; Zollman, "Nature of American Religious Corporations"—14 *Michigan Law Review* 37; Bouvier, *Law Dictionary,* ad v. "Corporation."

[69] Cf. canons 488, 4°; 684-725.

[70] *American Law:* In the United States all corporations must be constituted under the authority of the state. The American Law does not recognize the Church's right to create or constitute a corporate person which will be capable of enjoying civil corporate rights. These bodies must observe the same procedure as any lay or business association would in order to effect incorporation (Brown, *Juristic Personality,* p. 133). The status before the secular law of ecclesiastical corporations, duly incorporated in the civil sphere, is that they "are not to be regarded as ecclesiastical corporations, in the sense of English law, which were composed entirely of ecclesiastical persons, and subject to the ecclesiastical judicatories; but as belonging to the class of civil corporations to be controlled and managed according to the principle of common law as administered by the ordinary tribunals of justice" (Robertson v. Bullions, 11 N. Y. 243, 251, affirming 9 Barb. 64, 87; Calkins v. Cheney, 92 Ill. 463, 478). A "religious corporation" is a corporation created for religious purposes. "It is quite clear that in matters of an ecclesiastical nature relating to the government and discipline of a church, the decision of the constituted authorities of the church is final and is binding on the civil tribunals of justice" (Watson v. Jones, 13 Wall 679; Rector of St. James Church v. Huntington, 82 Hun. 125; Baxter v. McDermott, 155 N. Y. 83). Cf. Westminster Presbyterian Church v. Presbytery, 142 App. Div. 855, 127 N. Y. Supp. 836. All questions of faith, doctrine and discipline belong exclusively to the church and its spiritual officers.—Waller v. Howell, 20 Misc. 236, 45 N. Y. Supp. 790.

[71] Canon 99. Cf. Zollman, "Classes of American Religious Corporations"—13 *Michigan Law Review* 566.

religious are separate and distinct from the rights of the members, this writer does not subscribe to Roberti's view.

Roberti, while holding that the moral person as described does enjoy the privileged forum, nevertheless, maintains that there can be no possibility for the incurring of the censure under canon 2198 since in penal law every analogical application is ruled out inasmuch as no penalty becomes applicable as long as there is not verified the exact case of the law's violation for which the penalty is enacted. To this statement, a full agreement can readily be given.[72]

B. *Reserved Competence*

In Canon Law, competence differs from jurisdiction as a part differs from the whole: each judge has jurisdiction, but each, except the Supreme Pontiff, is by law barred from the exercise of a universal jurisdiction.[73]

Canon 1559, § 1, declares that no person can be sued in a court of first instance except before a judge or a tribunal endowed with due competence. Canon 1559, § 3, restates the general principle that the party convening must follow the forum of the party convened. Competence refers to that jurisdiction by which a judge or a tribunal is empowered to decide a particular case of a certain person in a determined place. This competence is determined in various ways, depending on the nature of the case, the persons involved in the suit, and the territory in which the defendant has his domicile or quasi-domicile.

Whether the collegiate moral person is a party plaintiff or a party defendant in a contentious case before an ecclesiastical court, the question of the competent forum is of paramount importance to it. It is true that the question of competence directly concerns the judge in the case, who is bound by canon 1609 to ascertain his competence before summoning the defendant in the case. But it is also important to the parties themselves, for canon 1892, 1°, de-

---

[72] Roberti, "*De Privilegio Fori*"—Apollinaris (Romae, 1928-), III (1930), 635-637, esp. p. 635.

[73] Coronata, *Institutiones*, III, n. 1093, p. 10; Regatillo, *Institutiones Iuris Canonici*, II, n. 339; Vermeersch-Creusen, *Epitome*, III, n. 10, p. 7.

clares that the sentence of an absolutely incompetent judge is voided by an irremediable nullity. Even relative competence has a direct bearing on the corporation's obligation, for example, on its obligation to answer a summons;[74] to submit to suit in a particular court, and to abide by the decision of that court, according to law.[75]

This writer will now discuss three phases of competence in ecclesiastical procedural law in so far as these phases affect the collegiate moral person. First, reserved competence; second, the necessary forum; finally, the ordinary forum.

The limitation of competency by reservation points simply to the exclusive or absolute competence of a particular judge or court. Since the Roman Pontiff has received from Christ supreme authority over the whole Church, it follows that he possesses full jurisdiction and all its attributes. He is the highest judge by whom all may be tried, and he is the supreme judge whom no one may try.[76]

He is the competent judge, even in the first instance, of all baptized persons, of all things and causes which look to the judicial forum of the Church for a decision or a settlement. His power is truly that of a primary jurisdiction.[77] From this right flows a principle which has been recognized since time immemorial, namely, the right on the part of all the faithful to appeal to the Holy See in any kind of a case and at any stage of the procedure, or also to take the case there in the first instance.[78]

But, although the Pope enjoys this universal jurisdiction, he nevertheless reserves to his own exclusive tribunal only certain cases which are called *causae maiores*.[79] There are certain tribunals which serve to spare the labor of the Holy Father. The judicial authority of the Roman Curia is vested in three tribunals, namely, the Sacred Penitentiary,[80] limited in its authority to the internal forum; the

---

[74] Canons 1559; 1714.
[75] Canon 1873.
[76] Canons 1556; 1557; cf. canon 1569.
[77] Canons 218-221.
[78] Canon 1569, § 1.
[79] Canons 220; 1557, § 1; 1600.
[80] Canon 258.

Sacred Roman Rota,[81] and the Apostolic Signatura,[82] authorized for their judicial cognizance in the external forum.

Of direct concern here is the Sacred Roman Rota. The Sacred Roman Rota consists of a certain number of prelates designated by the Supreme Pontiff who are called Auditors.[83] The Sacred Roman Rota has appellate jurisdiction and also original jurisdiction, i.e., jurisdiction in the first instance.[84] The usual procedure is that a case is first heard in the diocesan court where the bishop is *ex-officio* the judge.[85] But the Sacred Roman Rota is competent in the first instance not only in those cases which are mentioned in canon 1557, §§ 2, 3, but also in cases, including criminal ones, which the Pope, either at the request of the litigants or at his own behest (*motu proprio*), has summoned to himself in order to commit them to the judgment of the Rota. It may decide these cases also in the second or third instances, if there be need to do so, and if the rescript of the commission contains nothing to the contrary.[86]

The Sacred Roman Rota is likewise an ordinary tribunal constituted by the Holy See to receive appeals.[87] The Sacred Rota tries, in the second instance, cases which have been tried in the first instance in courts of local ordinaries and have then been brought immediately to the Holy See by way of appeal.[88] It tries, in the last instance, cases which have been tried by the same Sacred Roman Rota or in any other court in the second or further instances, and which have not become a closed judicial issue (*res adiudicata*).[89]

The reservation of competence declared by canon 1557, § 2, 1°, does not include the contentious cases of residential bishops if they represent a collegiate moral person under their jurisdiction. Moreover, while contentious cases of residential bishops are reserved exclusively to the tribunals of the Holy See in general, there are

---

[81] Canon 259.

[82] Canon 259.

[83] Canon 1598, § 1; Wernz-Vidal, *Ius Canonicum*, VI, n. 131, p. 115.

[84] Wernz-Vidal, *Ius Canonicum, loc. cit.;* canon 1599, § 2.

[85] Canon 1572.

[86] Canon 1599, § 2; Wernz-Vidal, *Ius Canonicum*, VI, n. 131, p. 115.

[87] Canon 1598.

[88] Canon 1599, § 1, 1°.

[89] Canon 1599, § 1, 2°.

certain excepted cases mentioned in canon 1572, § 2. This canon states that cases involving the rights or temporal property of bishops, the episcopal fund for the support of his table (*mensa*),[90] or the diocesan Curia, are to be referred with the consent of the bishop either to a collegiate tribunal of the diocese, or to the judge of the immediately superior court (*ad iudicem immediate superiorem*). Thus, while canon 1557, § 2, 1°, does not indicate the nature of the contentious cases which are reserved thereby, a comparison of the two canons here indicated, as well as the form of the preliminary drafts of the Code, tends to establish that the reservation affects only those cases in which the residential bishop defends his personal rights and property, and not those cases in which he represents a moral person in his diocese or territory.[91]

This point is important in the present discussion, for the term "residential bishop" as used in canon 1557, § 2, 1°, includes in law also the abbot and prelate nullius,[92] and also the vicar and prefect apostolic.[93] It seems that the term likewise includes the apostolic administrator and the vicar capitular.[94]

The above-mentioned term seems also to include the supreme moderators of exempt religious congregations or orders, and this, too, is important because of the specific included mention of exempt religious moral bodies in canon 1557, § 2, 2°.[95] Thus, with the

---

[90] Augustine (1872-1943) maintained (*Rights and Duties of Ordinaries* [St. Louis, Mo.: B. Herder & Co., 1924], 47) that, while formerly the *mensa* represented one-fourth of the revenues or income of each church in the diocese as yielding to the bishop his support, now, in the United States, since the Church must in general derive its revenues from the free contributions of the faith, the *cathedraticum* has apparently taken the place of the *mensa* as a means of support for the bishop's table. Augustine held that, though the *cathedraticum* does not in law exist as a canonical means for the support of the bishop, yet it represents the one practical means available in the United States of America.

[91] Roberti, *De Processibus,* I, n. 63, p. 185; Lega-Bartoccetti, *Commentarius,* I, 36; Roberti *(loc. cit.),* cites his *Schemata* [Typis Polyglottis Vaticanis, 1940] in support of his position (Schema D. c. 11, § 2; E. c. 11, § 2; F. c. 6, § 4; G. c. 6, § 4).

[92] Canon 215, § 2.

[93] Canon 294 § 1.

[94] Roberti, *De Processibus,* I, n. 63, p. 185.

[95] Cf. Roberti, *loc. cit.*

legal parity between the supreme moderators and the residential bishop duly established in the law, it may be logically concluded that the reservation of competence declared by canon 1557, § 2, 1°, does not include the contentious cases either of residential bishops or of the others mentioned, if they represent a corporation under their ruling power. This reservation, in other words, is concerned with the purely personal status of those who are comprised under the term "residential bishop," and hence does not affect them in their representative capacity, when as head of one or several corporate bodies they seek a judicial decision or settlement in any of the intermediate ecclesiastical tribunals.

But there is a reserved competence which belongs exclusively by law to the tribunals of the Apostolic See and which at the same time concerns the ecclesiastical corporation directly. Canon 1557, § 2, 2°, declares that these tribunals are competent to judge dioceses and other ecclesiastical moral persons immediately subject to the Roman Pontiff, such as exempt religious institutes,[96] monastic congregations,[97] and the like.

There is no doubt that this canon includes mention of the collegiate moral person. First of all the generic phrase "*persona moralis ecclesiastica*" is used in the canon, and secondly the moral persons which by way of example are listed in the canon are precisely such as have the nature of a collegiate moral person. The religious institute referred to in canon 1557, § 2, 2°, may be one in which the members take solemn or simple vows, as long as it has been withdrawn from the jurisdiction of the local ordinary.[98] Non-exempt religious institutes of pontifical approval are not included under the listing contained in canon 1557, § 2, 2°.[99]

It may be questioned by what reason moral persons, such as a

---

[96] Exempt religious institutes are such as have been withdrawn from the jurisdiction of the local ordinary. It is immaterial whether the members of the institutes are professed with solemn or with simple vows. Cf. canon 488, 1°.

[97] A monastic congregation implies a confederation of several independent monasteries under one and the same superior. Cf. canon 488, 2°.

[98] Canon 488, 2°.

[99] Cf. canon 488, 3°.

diocese, an ecclesiastical province,[100] or an exempt religious institute which is not subject to any superior intermediate to the Roman Pontiff,[101] can be said to have no superior below the Roman Pontiff. Each moral person just mentioned has respectively the residential bishop, the metropolitan bishop and the supreme moderator as its legitimate superior. Lega-Bartoccetti maintain that the answer is apparent, since the canon contemplates a judicial superior.[102]

Does the exclusive competence of the Sacred Roman Rota[103] apply to the corporate person whether the latter be plaintiff or defendant? Or, to present the question in a different way: Would the ecclesiastical corporation which receives mention in canon 1557, § 2, 2°, both as plaintiff or as defendant against a natural person or a moral person with a superior below the Roman Pontiff, have the right to have its case decided by the Sacred Roman Rota? Lega-Bartoccetti[104] and Roberti[105] are of the opinion that the ecclesiastical moral person does not enjoy this exclusive or reserved competence of the Sacred Roman Rota in the rôle of party plaintiff. Roberti bases his opinion on the general principle that the plaintiff must follow the forum of the defendant and thereby indicates that the reserved competence under discussion would be limited to the moral person only in the rôle of party defendant.[106]

This writer is of the opinion, however, that the ecclesiastical moral person enjoys this exclusive or reserved competence, under canon 1557, § 2, 2°, of the Sacred Roman Rota whether the moral person be plaintiff or defendant. In the first place, canon 1557, § 2, employs the general term "to judge" (*iudicare*) in reference to its

---

[100] The territory over which an archbishop exercises metropolitan jurisdiction, e.g., his own archdiocese and at least one suffragan diocese.—Attwater, *A Catholic Dictionary* (New York: The Macmillan Co., 1941), ad v. "Province." Cf. canons 215, § 1 and 272.

[101] Religious provinces, i.e., the divisions of a religious order which comprises all its houses and members in a given district, and religious institutes which have a superior below the Roman Pontiff are governed in the matter of judicial competence by the law of canon 1579, §§ 2, 3.

[102] Commentarius, I, 37.

[103] Cf. canon 1599, § 2.

[104] *Op. cit.*, I, p. 38, n. 6.

[105] *De Processibus,* I, n. 63, p. 187.

[106] Roberti, *ibidem.*

subdivisions. The general nature of the term in question does not admit of limitations. It can be applied, in other words, to cases set forth in the canon whether the moral person concerned is party plaintiff or party defendant.

In the second place, canon 1609, § 2, states that before a judge admits a plaintiff to plead his case, he is bound to ascertain whether the plaintiff has a right in law to sue. Since the ecclesiastical moral person referred to in canon 1557, § 2, 2°, is just that type of litigant with no judicial[107] superior below the Roman Pontiff, this writer believes that a tribunal, other than the tribunal of the Apostolic See, would be obligated to abstain from entertaining all such cases in view of canon 1557, § 2, 2°, and canon 1609, § 2, and that all such cases should be referred to the Holy See for judgment whether the moral person is plaintiff or defendant. In the cases referred to under canon 1557, § 2, 2°, all other judges than the Apostolic See are absolutely incompetent to hear the cause.[108]

C. *The Necessary Forum*

The word "forum" is a loan-word derived from the Latin. It signifies the act or fact by which relative judicial power is determined.[109] The plaintiff follows the forum of the defendant; if the defendant can point to various courts that are competent in the case, the plaintiff has the right to choose between the courts.[110] There are some cases which have a necessary forum.[111] Then the proper tribunal must be approached under grave obligation, but not under the pain of nullity, for all other judges are only relatively incompetent to hear and decide such cases.[112] The obligation of following the necessary forum rests on the plaintiff.[113] Cases per-

[107] Lega-Bartoccetti, *Commentarius,* I, 37.

[108] Canons 1558; 1892, 1°.

[109] Vermeersch-Creusen, *Epitome,* III, n. 16.

[110] Canon 1559, § 3.

[111] Cf. canon 1560.

[112] Canon 1559, § 2; Coronata, *Institutiones,* III, n. 1100; Wernz-Vidal, *Ius Canonicum,* VI, n. 51.

[113] Wernz-Vidal, *loc. cit.*

taining to a necessary forum will be considered only in so far as they may concern, directly or indirectly, the ecclesiastical forum.

The following cases have a necessary forum.

1. Actions *de spolio* must be brought before the local ordinary where the property is located.[114]

The nature of the action *de spolio,* or the replevin action, is to recover the possession of a specific object or chattel, or the quasi-possession[115] of a right, of which one has been deprived in any manner by force or stealth. The action will lie against the tortious doer who perpetrated the unlawful seizure or detention.[116] The purpose and effect of the action is to recover possession of the specific chattel or object with its fruits, or of the exercise of the right in question.[117]

In the replevin action, the plaintiff is obligated to plead and prove the fact of possession, quasi-possession, or simple tenure, but not of the ownership[118] of the chattel, thing or right in issue, and also the fact of the deprivation of it in an unlawful or wrongful way.[119] If rightful possession of the chattel or of the right in question does not belong legally to the plaintiff,[120] or if it is clear and evident by judicial sentence or from a public document that the defendant is the rightful owner, the plaintiff will have no right to recover the goods in law.[121]

---

[114] Canon 1560, 1°. An *actio de spolio* is the equivalent of a replevin suit.

[115] The term "quasi-possession" is used in the Code in the sense of rights possessed which are incorporeal in nature, for example, the right of election. Cf. canon 1668, §2.

[116] Canon 1698, § 1; Muñiz, *Procédimientos Eclesiásticos* (2. ed., 3 vols., Seville: Lib. de Sobrino de Izquierdo, 1926), III, n. 76; Coronata, *Institutiones,* III, n. 1228; Wernz, *Ius Decretalium,* V, n. 502.

[117] Reiffenstuel (lib. II, tit. XIII, nn. 104-155) pointed out that this restitution implied not only the restoration of the possession of the object or of the exercise of the right, but also of any income that had accrued since the spoliation had taken place. Cf. Noval, *De Iudiciis,* n. 365.

[118] Canon 1694; cf. Wernz-Vidal, *Ius Canonicum,* VI, n. 345.

[119] Canon 1698, § 1; 1694. Cf. also Muñiz, *Procédimientos Eclesiásticos,* III, n. 79; Roberti, *De Processibus,* I, n. 273; Wernz-Vidal, *Ius Canonicum,* VI, n. 352.

[120] Cf., for example, canons 1442; 1439, § 1; 2294, §1; 2413, § 1.

[121] Coronata, *Institutiones,* III, n. 1228; Noval, *De Iudiciis,* n. 365, p. 258; Wernz-Vidal, *Ius Canonicum,* VI, n. 357.

A defendant who has been the victim of a spoliation may claim an *exceptio spolii.* This is a dilatory exception which tends to retard the progress of a case or a trial rather than to defeat it. The effect of the exception of spoliation when invoked by the defendant in a trial would be that he is not bound to put in an answer in the case in question until the chattel or object has been returned to his possession.[122]

According to canon 1495, § 2, legal entities which have been created as juridical persons by ecclesiastical authority have the right to acquire, own and administer temporal goods according to the laws of the sacred canons. It is easily conceivable that an ecclesiastical corporation could need to have recourse to this type of action. The corporation may be the possessor of various movable and immovable properties, the loss of which may be incurred through the wrongful act of another.

2. Cases concerning a benefice, even though it be not a residential one, must be tried before the local ordinary where the benefice exists.[123]

This provision of ecclesiastical law may likewise apply to a corporate body in the Church. For example, under canon 1425 parishes may be united with houses of religious. A religious house itself is a collegiate moral person;[124] a parish, on the other hand, is a benefice, and although it is composed of the faithful, it is, according to the accepted teaching of the canonists, a non-collegiate moral person.[125]

---

[122] Canons 1698, §§ 1, 2; 1699, § 1; Coyle, *Judicial Exceptions,* The Catholic University of America Canon Law Studies, n. 193 (Washington, D. C.: The Catholic University of America Press, 1944), p. 7.

[123] Canon 1560, 2°.

[124] Regatillo, *Institutiones Iuris Canonici,* I, n. 202. The term "religious house" here means, not the physical dwelling, but the religious community of at least three physical persons. Cf. c. 100, § 2.

[125] Regatillo, *loc. cit.;* Wernz-Vidal, *Ius Canonicum,* II, n. 28. Cf., however, Hannan, "Parochial Ownership"—*The Homiletic and Pastoral Review* (New York, 1900-), XLII (1941), 255-267. Cf. also "The Juridical Status of the Parishes of Religious"—*The Jurist* (Washington, D. C.: 1941-), I (1941), 329-335. *American Law.* There were two distinct, prevalent theories or views of what constitutes a religious body corporate in the State of New York. According to one of those views the society itself does not

If, then, a parish is united by the Holy See with a religious house with respect to the temporalities only, then the religious house has only the right to the revenues of the parish and the right to present a priest of the secular clergy to the bishop of the diocese to be instituted as pastor. On the other hand, if a parish is united with a religious house in full right (*pleno iure*), it becomes a religious parish, and the superior has the right to nominate a priest of his religious institute for the care of souls, with the right reserved to the local ordinary to examine and install him in office.[126]

Now, any case concerning a parish so united to a corporation would, since the parish is a benefice, have to be brought before the ordinary of the place where the benefice is located, for there the necessary forum exists. Such a case could concern the transfer of the benefice,[127] or also the division and the dismemberment of the parish in question.[128] And, if the benefice were non-parochial in nature, then any judicial action attending its proposed conversion to a parochial benefice would likewise be brought before the court of the local ordinary.[129] These are but a few of the possible questions that could call for a judicial decision or settlement in the court which is constituted as the necessary forum.

3. The third class of cases which have a necessary forum are those concerning administration, which are to be tried before the local ordinary of the place where the administration was conducted.[130]

---

become incorporated, but only its trustees. The other view, and the now accepted one in the State of New York, assumes that the society itself is incorporated; that the "previous voluntary association" is merged in the corporation, as far as its secular affairs are concerned. The trustees, under this second opinion, are not the body corporate itself, but merely its officers. The members of the association form the constituent body or the corporation.—Robertson v. Bullions (1854), 11 N. Y. 243. Cf. Gram v. Prussia Emigrated Evangelical Lutheran German Society (1867), 36 N. Y. 161; People v. Keese (1882), 27 Hun. 483; Watkins v. Wilcox (1875), 4 Hun. 220, affirmed (1876), 66 N. Y. 654; Wyatt v. Benson (1857), 23 Barb. 327.

126 Canon 1425; cf. also, canons 452; 1423, § 2; Wernz-Vidal, *Ius Canonicum*, II, n. 170.

127 Canon 1426.

128 Canon 1427.

129 Canon 1430, § 2.

130 Canon 1560, 3°.

This forum concerns administration in its broad sense. It concerns public or private administration, and includes all acts whether performed by a physical or by a moral person. No distinction should be made when the law itself does not invoke any distinction.[131] It would include, therefore, all acts, whether the suit concerns the administrator as plaintiff against the persons for whom the administration is carried out, or vice versa.[132]

However, by far the more important and vital phase of administration which could involve the need of a judicial process, and hence call for the application of the law as enacted in canon 1560, 3°, is the act of administration which concerns ecclesiastical property or church goods. For the present, the matter immediately to be discussed is the nature of this special kind of administration and the proper identification and determination of those who have the power of administration. To have seen these matters in some detail will furnish means of more easily interpreting the canon now being considered, at least in one of its major parts, and a part which concerns the ecclesiastical corporation to a very great extent.

By *ecclesiastical goods* are meant the temporal goods, whether movable or immovable, and the temporal rights which belong to the universal Church, or to the Apostolic See, or to any other moral person in the Church.[133]

In Title XXVIII of Book Three of the Code[134] the law for the administration of ecclesiastical goods is set down. The goods of religious institutes are not directly treated under this title; they are treated in a special chapter in that part of the Code which deals especially with the laws for religious.[135]

A. *Definition and Classification of Administration.* Administration is defined as the management or control of the temporal goods of the Church for the purpose of serving the ends for which these goods or properties were acquired. This definition of necessity includes all acts necessary for preserving the property in good repair

---

[131] Lega-Bartoccetti, *Commentarius,* I, 48, n. 13.

[132] Roberti, *De Processibus,* I, n. 65.

[133] Canon 1497, § 1.

[134] Canons 1518-1528.

[135] Canons 531-537. These canons contain cross references to canons 1518-1528.

and for making it productive. The definition does not overlook the fact that the best use should be derived from the property and that a beneficial application of the goods for their legitimate purposes should be made.[136] Administration may be divided into acts of ordinary and into acts of extraordinary administration.[137]

Acts of ordinary administration may be said to be those acts which the administrator can perform validly by reason of his office and without the permission of his superior.[138] When the law demands that certain administrative acts be done only with the permission of the competent superior in order that these acts may be placed validly, then these acts are of an extraordinary character.[139] When such a permission from the superior is required beforehand for the performance of a valid act of administration, the law usually contemplates a special condition or transaction such as an act of alienation.[140]

Administration may be either of an immediate or of a mediate type. The mediate type relates to the supreme power of the pope[141]

---

[136] Comyns, *Papal and Episcopal Administration of Church Property,* The Catholic University of America Canon Law Studies, n. 147 (Washington, D. C.: The Catholic University of America Press, 1942), p. 1.

[137] Cf. canon 1527.

[138] Comyns, *op. et loc. cit.*

[139] Blat, *Commentarium,* Lib. III, Pars II-VI, 540; Vromant *De Bonis Ecclesiae Temporalibus* (2. ed., Louvain: Museum Lessianum, 1934), pp. 195-196; De Meester, *Compendium Juris Canonici et Juris Canonico-Civilis* (nova editio, 3 vols. in 4, Brugis; Desclée De Brouwer, 1921-1928, Tom. III, Pars I, n. 1479, p. 399 (hereafter cited *Compendium*).

[140] Canons 1530-1533. "Alienation is any act or contract whereby church property is exposed to danger of loss, or its legal possession is reduced to a worse condition. It is that act by which property, real rights, or possession of any ecclesiastical moral person are gratuitously or onerously transferred, set aside, lessened, or burdened."—Cleary, *Canonical Limitations on the Alienation of Church Property,* The Catholic University of America Canon Law Studies, n. 100 (Washington, D. C.: The Catholic University of America, 1936), p. 2.

[141] This supreme power includes the direct administration over any and all moral persons within the Church, since the pope has ordinary and immediate power of jurisdiction over them.—Pistocchi, *De Bonis Ecclesiae Temporalibus* (Taurini: Marietti, 1932), p. 71; Vermeersch-Creusen, *Epitome,* II, 520.

over all ecclesiastical property in the Church,[142] as well as the supervisory power[143] of the local ordinary, and of those who are equivalent to him in law,[144] over all ecclesiastical property within the diocese or territory.

However, within the purpose of this dissertation to exemplify the term "administration" in canon 1560, 3°, in so far as it relates to or concerns the collegiate moral person in the Church, the writer limits the discussion to some, if not all, of those acts of immediate administration which are connected with temporalities within the ordinary or extraordinary power of the administrator who by the general or the particular law, by the constitutions of the moral body or by laudably established custom, is disputed for these acts of administration.

B. *Immediate Administration.* With the term immediate administration the writer points to a direct management and control of ecclesiastical property.

a) *By the Local Ordinary.* The local ordinary possesses certain rights of immediate administration. This dissertation is primarily concerned with collegiate moral persons. Accordingly, if mention is made only of these in relation to the sources of immediate administration of the local ordinary, it is not to be supposed that the local ordinary possesses only these and no other powers within the scope of his administration.

Canon 1182, § 1, safeguards the administration of church property in general, as governed by canons 1519-1528. The canon then declares to whom pertains the administration of the goods which are destined for the repair and the embellishment of the churches, and for the divine service at cathedral, collegiate and other churches.[145] In a cathedral church the administration of these goods

---

[142] Coronata, *Institutiones,* II, n. 1059; Vromant, *De Bonis Ecclesiae Temporalibus,* pp. 202-203.

[143] Canon 1519, § 1.

[144] Cf. canon 198, § 1.

[145] A collegiate church is "one served by a college of secular priests, called canons, because they form a chapter and sometimes live in common." There are no such churches in England now, but they are still found on the continent, especially in Italy.—Attwater, *A Catholic Dictionary,* ad v. "Collegiate Church."

belongs to the bishop and the chapter conjointly. Therefore both the bishop and the chapter need the consent of each other before anything concerning the administration can be validly done.[146]

In dioceses or territories which have no cathedral chapters the co-administration of the cathedral church does not devolve on the body of diocesan consultors[147] which must be constituted by the local ordinary in the place of the chapter; nor does the advisory council of missionary priests (*consilium missionariorum*)[148] hold the place of the cathedral chapter.[149]

Other administrators besides the local ordinary which are authorized and designated by the Code are the following persons, in so far as they are collegiate moral persons or concern them.

b) *By Chapters.* The chapter acts as a whole in the administration of the property which belongs to the chapter and to the cathedral or the collegiate church. It is evident that the chapter is the administrator for the properties aforementioned.[150] Since the chapter, according to canon 415, has the right to administer the property of the cathedral church even when such a church is also a parochial church, *a fortiori* the chapter has the right when the church is not parochial, but only collegiate, in character.

In all other cases pertinent to the present discussion the Code does not directly designate the administrators of the properties and possessions of collegiate moral persons, but gives to these juristic persons the right and power to choose their own particular administrators, who are sanctioned as such by law.[151]

---

[146] S.R.R., *Causa Corduben. in America,* 1 feb. 14, 1915—*AAS,* VII (1915), 131-133.

[147] In the United States the cathedral chapter has not been constituted. Cf. Klekotka, *Diocesan Consultors,* The Catholic University of America Canon Law Studies, n. 8 (Washington, D. C.: The Catholic University of America, 1920), p. 12. Since the body of diocesan consultors exists in the place of the cathedral chapter, it may be contended that, like cathedral chapters, the body of diocesan consultors is constituted as a collegiate moral person. But this view of the nature of the body of diocesan consultors as such is not accepted by all authors. Cf. Klekotka, *op. cit.,* pp. 29-36. Klekotka holds that the diocesan consultors form a collegiate moral person.

[148] Canon 302.

[149] Comyns, *Papal and Episcopal Administration of Church Property,* p. 93.

[150] Couly, *Les Biens Temporals de l'Eglise"—Le Canoniste Contemporain* (Paris, 1878-1922), XLV (1922), 403-404.

[151] Coronata, *Institutiones,* II, n. 1062.

c) *By other Administrators.* These administrators may be classified as follows: i. Those persons who are authorized by the particular constitutions of religious institutes and also of societies of men and women who live the community life without vows.[152] ii. The duly elected officers of lay associations which have been constituted moral persons according to law, who administer the common property of such associations.[153] iii. Administrators designated by particular law or statute which has been duly approved by the competent superior.

The acts and interest, rights and liabilities, attributed to ecclesiastical corporations by law[154] are those of natural or physical persons. Otherwise the body of corporate law would be void of any relation to actual fact and of any serious end. The corporate concept involves some physical person or persons whose interests are attributed to the corporation, and some physical person or persons whose acts are imputed to the corporation. A corporation, lacking body and soul, cannot act except through an agency of some representative or administrator, who is evidently necessary for the control and management of corporate affairs.[155] Legal acts of the corporation can be performed only through agents or administrators.

For like reasons, a corporation can have no interests, and therefore no rights, except those which are attributed to it as trustee[156]

---

[152] Cf. canons 532, § 2; 676, § 2.

[153] Canons 691; 697, § 1.

[154] Cf. canon 100.

[155] Brown, *Juristic Personality,* p. 99.

[156] This term is used not without some misgivings. The relationship between a corporation and its beneficiaries may or may not amount to a trust in the strict sense. Membership in a corporation is not the beneficial ownership of a certain proportion of the corporate property (cf. canons 1495; 1501. Also, Doheny, *Practical Problems in Church Finance* [Milwaukee: The Bruce Publishing Co., 1941], pp. 24, 30), but the benefit of a contract, made by the member with the corporation under which he is to receive certain benefits of a temporal or spiritual nature, under the law. Cf. canons 707-709; 713; 722; 1499; 1500; 1501.

For example, it is the unanimous opinion of canonists that religious profession is a contract between the religious and the corporation. Cf. Schaefer, *De Religiosis ad Normam Codicis Canonici* (3. ed., Romae: S. A.L.E.R., 1940), n. 263; Coronata, *Institutiones,* I, n. 589; Pejska, *Ius Canonicum*

for or on behalf of actual physical persons. These actual persons are called the beneficiaries. Whatever a corporation is reputed to do in law is done in fact by the administrators or members, as representatives, of the corporation. Whatever interests, rights or property it possesses in law[157] are in fact those of its immediate members, within the scope and limit of its rights of administration of ecclesiastical property, as has been set forth above, and these interests, rights and property are held by it for their immediate benefit.[158]

Every ecclesiastical collegiate person, therefore, has corresponding to it in the world of physical persons certain agents or representatives by whom it acts. In some matters the collegiate person may be represented by administrators authorized to act in their own name and according to their own discretion.[159] The acts of these representatives done within the scope of their authority is looked upon as the act of the corporation itself. But the corporation may also act in a collegiate manner. There are two possible types of questions which may come before the collegiate body for decision, namely, those which affect each member individually and those which do not. The collegiate procedure, in these respective matters, will depend on the question before the corporation.

There are rights which are proper to the corporate entity as such, for instance, corporate property; and there are also rights which radically and vitally affect each member as such. It is to

---

Religiosorum (3. ed., Friburgi-Brisgoviae: Herder, 1927), p. 103; Chelodi, *Ius Canonicum de Personis*, p. 240; Wernz-Vidal, *Ius Canonicum*, III, 262; Vermeersch-Creusen, *Epitome*, I, 519. This contract is a bilateral contract in a proper but less strict sense, i.e., it obliges both parties and is to the advantage of both, prescinding from the question whether the parties are equal in right, and hence whether they are bound by the terms of the contract in communitative justice. Cf. Cavagnis, *Institutiones Iuris Publici Ecclesiastici* (4. ed., 3 vols., Romae, 1906), I, p. 419, n. 662.

[157] Canons 100, §§ 1, 3; 1495, § 2.

[158] The various Church institutions are independent subjects of rights and duties. If one of these bodies is dissolved or ceases to exist, the property passes to the immediately higher ecclesiastical moral person, subject always to the will and intentions of the founders and benefactors, to lawfully acquired rights, and to the special laws which govern the extinct person.—Canon 1501.

[159] Ayrinhac, *General Legislation in the New Code of Canon Law* (New York, 1923), p. 216.

this latter type that the legal maxim, "Quod autem omnes, uti singulos, tangit, ab omnibus probari debet,"[160] refers. The holding of an election through specially deputized representatives[161] would have to be unanimously agreed upon.[162] Instances in which an additional personal obligation is imposed, as an assessment, also require unanimous consent.[163]

The ordinary mode of corporate acting in matters not affecting the individuals as such is set forth in canon 101, § 1, 1°. At this point the purpose of this dissertation does not demand an exemplification of the law concerning this particular procedure. It suffices to understand that the juridical person has certain agents or administrators by whom it acts and that it, the corporation, may itself act in a collegiate manner requiring one of two modes of procedure depending on the question involved.

The corporate representatives may or may not be persons different from its beneficiaries, for these two capacities are not incompatible. In a purely charitable corporation, the beneficiaries may have no interest whatever in the management of its affairs.

Lastly, it is worthy of notice that some or all of the members of an ecclesiastical corporation may themselves be corporations. For example, the *congregatio monastica* is a confederation of several independent monasteries under one and the same superior.[164] In this type of corporation the entity is none the less dependent on physical persons who must act for it.

What cases, then, in respect to moral persons, are comprehended by the act of administration determining, under canon 1560, 3°, the forum for their adjudication?

There seems to be no doubt that all acts of administration, either public or private, by which the affairs of a physical or moral person are managed, are included under that term of administration used in canon 1560, 3°. When the law itself does not distinguish,

---

[160] Canon 101, § 1, 2°. The wording of this canon is plainly an adaptation of Reg. 29, R.J., in VI°, which reads: "Quod omnes tangit, debet ab omnibus approbari."

[161] Blat, *Commentarium*, Lib. II, Pars I, 40.

[162] Canon 172, § 1.

[163] Blat, *Commentarium*, *loc. cit.*

[164] Canon 488, 2°.

no distinction should be made. The law of this canon is based on pre-Code law, and according to canon 6, n. 6, it must therefore be interpreted in accordance with pre-Code law.[165]

The necessary forum is constituted for acts of administration, since the administration is authorized by a contract or quasi-contract[166] between the administrator and another or others either expressly or tacitly commissioning the office of administration. These parties are considered, from the prescript of the law itself, to have elected the place of trial where the administration is carried out, inasmuch as the trial can progress more easily and expeditiously at that place.[167]

Since this forum rests on the tacit renunciation, by the parties to a contract, of the ordinary forum based, for example, on domicile or the situs of property, this forum for acts of administration is necessarily limited to the parties to the contract or those for whose benefit it was made, and does not extend to third parties or strangers to that contract. So, for example, whether the corporate person is plaintiff or defendant in a suit in which the other party is either the administrator, a beneficiary or a member, the proper place for the trial is before the local ordinary of the place where the act of administration in question was performed. On the other hand, when the corporation is plaintiff or defendant and the other party to the suit is a third party or stranger to the contract aforementioned, then the suit must be brought before the competent court according to the ordinary rules of procedure.[168]

Canon 1529 declares that the civil law of a nation or state on contracts and payments of all kinds is to be observed by Canon Law in matters ecclesiastical, except in so far as the civil law is contrary to the divine law, or Canon Law rules to the contrary. In short, the Church adopts the civil law of the different nations for contracts

---

[165] Roberti, *De Processibus,* I, n. 65; *Coronata, Institutiones,* III, n. 1101; Lega-Bartoccetti, *Commentarius,* I, 48, n. 13.

[166] In the more proper and strict sense, quasi-contract can be defined as a unilateral act, voluntarily placed, in circumstances to which the law attaches the sanction of an obligation that binds. Cf. Heylen, *De Iure et Iustitia* (4. ed., 2 vols., Mechlinae: H. Dessain, 1943), I, 166.

[167] Canon 1565, § 2. Lega-Bartoccetti, *Commentarius,* I, 48, 13; Roberti, *De Processibus,* I, n. 65.

[168] Lega-Bartoccetti, *loc. cit.*

concerning ecclesiastical goods and rights connected with them. Now the question arises: Would cases concerning the administration of such contracts which fall under canon 1529 be heard and decided according to the norm of civil law even as to the matter pertaining to judicial competence? Lega-Bartoccetti are of the opinion that these cases relative to the matter of judicial competence, fall under the Canon Law, since there is a saving clause in canon 1529, namely, ". . . *nisi aliud iure canonico caveatur,*" and canon 1560, 3°, provides the competent forum for such cases.[169] This opinion seems to the writer to be a correct view of the law, and indeed for the very reason here submitted in vindication thereof.

4. The fourth class of cases which have a necessary forum are those concerning pious bequests or legacies. Such cases must be tried before the local ordinary of the domicile of the testator, except the question should turn about the mere execution of a legacy or bequest, which is to be settled according to the ordinary rules of competency.[170]

D. *The Ordinary Forum*

Besides the norms which relate to the extraordinary forums and the necessary forums, there are various ordinary norms in the law which indicate the selecting of the proper forum of the defendant.[171]

The general rule for the determining of competency is based on territorial limits.[172] Of the ordinary titles, in accordance with this rule, by which a defendant comes under the jurisdiction of a particular court, the first and most natural is the one of domicile.[173] Canon 1561, § 1, declares that by reason of domicile or quasi-domicile any person may be summoned as defendant before the ordinary of the place. A domicile may be acquired in two ways: (1) by staying in a parish, diocese or some such place with the intention of remaining permanently unless one be called away; and

---

[169] Lega-Bartoccetti, *Commentarius,* I, 49, n. 14.

[170] Canon 1560, 4°.

[171] Canons 1561-1568.

[172] Król, *The Defendant in Contentious Trials,* p. 63.

[173] Canon 1561, § 1.

(2) by remaining in a place for a full period of ten years.[174] A quasi-domicile may likewise be acquired in two ways: (1) by staying in a place with the intention of remaining beyond a period of six months unless one be called away; and (2) by a stay which is actually protracted beyond six months.[175]

According to some authors,[176] the moral person enjoys a proper domicile in the same manner as a physical person;[177] likewise, at least if the moral person is collegiate, also a quasi-domicile (for example, a monastery which has been closed for a time and transferred to another place, where it has remained over six months the while the intention of returning to its former site was never relinquished.[178] Other authors, on the contrary, deny that a moral person is competent to have a domicile or quasi-domicile in the strict sense of these words.[179]

This controversy seems to be rather about a name than about the thing itself.[180] For the purpose of this dissertation the question need not be treated in detail. It is certain that the moral person has a juridical seat (*sedem*), on which account it is subjected to the particular law of a determined place and by which the acquisition and exercise of its rights are determined, such as, for example, that which concerns the forum in canon 1560, 2°, 3°.[181] But these

---

174 Canon 92, § 1.

175 Canon 92, § 2.

176 Coronata, *Institutiones,* I, n. 129; Maroto, *Institutiones Iuris Canonici* (2 vols., Matriti, 1918-1919), I, nn. 410, 415, ad 3 (hereafter cited *Institutiones*).

177 Maroto (*Institutiones,* I, n. 410) holds that the domicile of the moral person should be called juridical.

178 Maroto, *Institutiones,* I, n. 412, ad (d); Coronata, *Institutiones,* I, n. 129.

179 Costello, *Domicile and Quasi-Domicile,* The Catholic University of America Canon Law Studies, n. 60 (Washington, D. C: The Catholic University of America, 1930), p. 172; Laurin, "Wesen und Bedeutung des Domizils"—*Archiv für katholisches Kirchenrecht,* XXVI (1871), p. 184, § 10; Vindex, "Domicilium et Quasi-Domicilium"—*Jus Pontificum* (Romae, 1921-) VI (1926), n. 33, p. 44, and n. 52, p. 53; Gillet, *La Personalité Juridique,* p. 255.

180 Michiels, *Principia Generalia de Personis in Ecclesia* (Lublin: Universitas Catholica, 1932), p. 176.

181 Michiels, *op. cit.,* pp. 176-177; Gillet, *op. cit.,* p. 255; cf. Vindex, "art. cit," *loc. cit.;* Costello, *op. cit.,* p. 172.

seats are improperly called domiciles or quasi-domiciles, for they are at most merely analogical domiciles or quasi-domiciles, for the constitutive elements of domicile and quasi-domicile, as enumerated in canon 92, are properly applicable to physical persons only, and the juridical effects of canon 94, § 1, are applied to moral persons for a different reason.[182] To this view, held by Michiels, the writer subscribes.

Where do corporations, then, have their seat or domicile, posited the analogical sense of the term? These juristic persons have a domicile in the place where they were constituted or erected.[183] And in that place these corporations may be sued before the local ordinary in accordance with canon 1561, § 1.[184]

To cite one example, a legitimately constituted house of three or more religious is a collegiate moral person,[185] and as such is by nature perpetual.[186] It cannot exist, therefore, except in a place where the religious community has a fixed and abiding residence. This is of the essence of its erection or constitution, and it is from this place of erection that its juridical seat, or domicile, is legally determined. Hence, a group of religious who by reason of persecution, war or accident, take up their abode in a place without the intention of establishing a domicile there, at least of prolonging their sojourn, cannot constitute a juridical house.[187] This mark of

---

[182] Michiels, *op. cit.*, p. 177; *Vindex*, "art. cit," *loc. cit.;* Gillet, *op. et loc. cit.*

[183] Michiels, *op. cit.*, pp. 176-177; Gillet, *op. cit.*, p. 255; Coronata, *Institutiones*, III, n. 1102; Wernz-Vidal, *Ius Canonicum*, VI, n. 54; Muñiz, *Procédimientos Eclesiásticos*, III, n. 206. The same principle was recognized in the pre-Code law. Gregory XVI (1831-1846) held (*Bullarii Romani Continuatio Summorum Pontificum*, XIX (1857), Parte III, tit. II, sezione 1 (Reg. Greg.), § 440): "Le azioni fra soci, dipendenti dai contratti di società, e quelle contro i soci, per causa della società finchè essa dura, saranno introdotte avanti il tribunale del luogo ove esiste il principale stabilimento della medesima." Cf. Vindex, "art. cit," *Jus Pontificium*, VI (1926), n. 33, p. 44, and n. 52, p. 53.

[184] Michiels, *op. cit.*, p. 177; Coronata, *Institutiones*, III, n. 1102; Wernz-Vidal, *Ius Canonicum*, VI, n. 54; Muñiz, *Procédimientos Eclesiásticos*, III, n. 206.

[185] Canon 100, §§ 1, 2.

[186] Canon 102, § 1.

[187] Larraona, "Commentarium Codicis"—*Commentarium pro Religiosis* (Romae, 1920—; later [1935] *Commentarium pro Religiosis et Missionariis*), III (1922), 48 (hereafter cited *CpR*).

stability constitutes the legal domicile, or the juridical seat, for the juridical person, so that in accordance with canon 1561, § 1, it may be sued before the local ordinary of the place where that seat or domicile is situated.[188]

[188] *American Law*: If the term domicile can apply to corporations, they have their domicile wherever they are created—City of St. Louis v. Ferry Co., 40 Mo. 580; cf. North and South Rolling Stock Co. v. People, 147 Ill. 234, 35 N.E. 608, 24 L. R. A. 462. This holds true irrespective of the residences of the officers or the place where the business is transacted.—Merrick v. Van Santvoord, 34 N. Y. 208; cf. Austin v. Telephone Co., 73 Hun. 96, 25 N. Y. Supp. 916.

A corporation, if incorporated under the laws of a state which is divided into more than one federal district, is a citizen and *inhabitant* of that district within which the general business of the corporation is done, and where it has its headquarters and general offices.—Galveston &c R. Co. v. Gonzales (1893) 151 U. S. 496, 38 L.Ed. 248.

In 1809, Chief Justice Marshall said: "That name (corporation), indeed, can not be an alien or a citizen; but the persons whom it represents may be the one or the other; and the controversy is, in fact and in law, between those persons suing in their corporate character."—Bank of United States v. Deveaux, 5 Cranch (U. S.) 61, at p. 87.

In 1861, Chief Justice Taney said in Ohio &c. R. Co. v. Wheeler, 1 Black. (U. S.) 286, 17 L. Ed. 130 at p. 296: "This question, as to the character of a corporation, and the jurisdiction of the courts of the United States, in cases wherein they were sued, or brought suit in their corporate name, was again brought before the court in the case of the Louisville, Cincinnati and Charleston R. Co. v. Letson, reported in 2 How. (U. S.) 497; and the court in that case, upon full consideration, decided, that where a corporation is created by the laws of a state, the legal presumption is, that its members are citizens of the State in which alone the corporate body has a legal existence; and that a suit by or against a corporation, in its corporate name, must be presumed to be a suit by or against citizens of the State which created the corporate body; and that no averment or evidence to the contrary is admissible, for the purpose of withdrawing the suit from the jurisdiction of a court of the United States." So, in the federal jurisdiction, the Deveaux, *supra,* was reversed for all practical purposes.

In general, the proper place for trial in the Supreme Court of the State of New York for domestic corporations, other than railroad companies, is in the county of their residence, namely, where they have their principal office as fixed by their certificate of incorporation, and also in counties where they have branch offices and transact part of their business.—Levey v. Payne, 200 App. Div. 30; 192 N. Y. Supp. 346, and cases cited; General Baking Co. v. Daniell, 181 App. Div. 501; 170 N. Y. Supp. 365; Poland v. United Transaction Co., 88 App. Div. 281; 85 N. Y. Supp., affd in 77 N. Y. 557.

Besides the ordinary forum of domicile, or, more properly, the forum of the corporate residence, the ecclesiastical corporation can for various reasons become subject to the jurisdiction of courts which are outside of the territory of its residence.

When the defendant is a foreign[189] ecclesiastical corporation, the court's authority to maintain the action, under the norms of the ordinary forum, depends on the nature of the suit. A foreign or non-resident corporation can be sued in an action *in rem*[190] directed against it before the local ordinary of the place where the litigious object, whether movable or immovable, is permanently located or situated.[191] According to canon 1564, a corporation can also summon a party before the local ordinary of the place where the litigious matter is situated. Such an action is real, not personal, in its character.

By reason of a contract, a corporation can sue and be sued before the ordinary of the place where the contract was made or where it is to be executed.[192] If the defendant is a non-resident or foreign corporation in the place where the contract was made or where it is to be executed, it cannot be sued there unless a stipulation to that effect was made at the time the contract was entered into.[193]

---

[189] This term is used here to signify an ecclesiastical corporation not having a residence in the ecclesiastical judicial territory where the trial is held.

[190] An action against the property itself, whether it be movable or immovable, which is permanently located in the court's territory, rather than an action against the person.—Cf. Augustine, *A Commentary,* VII, 20.

[191] Canon 1564.

[192] Canon 1565.

[193] The Pontifical Commission for the Authentic Interpretation of the Code was asked whether, according to canon 1565, § 1, a party can be sued on a contract before the ordinary of the place where the contract was made or where it is to be performed, even if he has left that place? The reply was given in the negative, without prejudice however to the provisions of canon 1565, § 2.—*AAS,* XIV (1922), 529; translation from Bouscaren, *The Canon Law Digest* (2 vols., Milwaukee, Bruce, 1934-1943), I, 741. If no stipulation was made in the contract, then the proper place for trial will be determined according to the other norms of judicial competency.

E. *The Competent Forum for Specific Religious Corporations*

The jurisdiction of religious tribunals[194] in the first instance relates to both contentious and criminal cases.[195] The writer is limiting the discussion here to contentious cases in which ecclesiastical corporations of religious are concerned. He will in a subsequent chapter consider the criminal actions involving these moral persons.

The contentious actions of ecclesiastical religious corporations, whether in the rôle of plaintiff or of defendant, which may be brought before the religious tribunal or the local ordinary's court of the first instance fall into four divisions: 1) Cases between said corporations of the same exempt clerical institute; 2) actions between said corporations of different exempt clerical institutes; 3) cases between said corporations of the same non-exempt or lay religious institute; and 4) actions between said corporations and secular clerics, lay persons, or lay moral persons (non-religious, but erected by ecclesiastical authority).

1) *Cases between ecclesiastical religious corporations of the same exempt clerical institute.* Unless the constitutions[196] prescribe otherwise, canon 1579, § 2, declares that in a controversy between two provinces, the supreme moderator of the institute judges the case in the first instance either in person or through a delegate; if the controversy is between two monasteries, the presiding abbot of the monastic congregation is the judge. While paragraph two of canon 1579 does not expressly mention "clerical" religious, it is easily deduced that its application is limited to clerical religious.

The religious province mentioned in this canon is defined by the Code[197] as the union of a number of religious houses which under one superior constitute a part of the same religious institute. The religious province is a collegiate moral person.[198] The houses

[194] Canon 1579, § 2.

[195] Roberti, *De Processibus,* I, n. 73.

[196] The religious institute or order requires, of necessity, constitutions, rules or by-laws by which the ends of the society and its government can be better achieved, in so far as the Code does not determine these matters in particular. Cf. Coronata, *Institutiones,* I, n. 501.

[197] Canon 488, 6°.

[198] Regatillo, *Institutiones Iuris Canonici,* I, n. 202; Wernz-Vidal *Ius Canonicum,* III, nn. 43, 65; Beste, *Introductio in Codicem,* p. 311; Schaefer, *De Religiosis,* n. 45.

of religious which constitute the province are not autonomous (*sui iuris*).[199] This distinguishes the province from the monastic congregation, for the latter confederation is composed of autonomous monasteries.[200] A province likewise is not *sui iuris,* whereas the monastic congregation is *sui iuris.*[201]

The case mentioned in the canon under discussion is the one that arises between two provinces of the same exempt clerical institute.[202] The institute involved is one composed of religious, mostly priests, of either solemn or simple vows, and one that has been withdrawn from the jurisdiction of the local ordinary.[203] The autonomous monastery or the monastery *sui iuris* here in question is one that is composed of men religious of solemn vows,[204] and one that is ruled by a superior elected by the monastery, according to the particular law of the institute. It has, besides the Roman Pontiff, no other ordinary superior with internal governing power.[205]

The judge in the first instance, therefore, in a suit between two provinces of the same institute, as just qualified, is the supreme moderator of the institute or his delegate.[206]

If the case is between two autonomous monasteries of the same exempt clerical institute, the presiding abbot of the monastic congregation is the judge.[207]

2) *Actions between corporations of different exempt clerical institutes.* When a controversy arises between two corporations of different exempt clerical institutes or societies, or between two monasteries of different monastic congregations, then, if at least one of these corporations has no judicial superior below the Roman Pontiff, it seems that the competency to judge the dispute will be reserved to the tribunals of the Holy See, according to canon 1557,

[199] Schaefer, *op. cit.,* n. 45.

[200] Schaefer, *op. cit.,* n. 41. a.

[201] Schaefer, *op. cit.,* n. 45.

[202] Lega-Bartoccetti, *Commentarius,* I, 139, n. 5; Wernz-Vidal, *Ius Canonicum,* VI, n. 93.

[203] Canon 488, 2°, 4°.

[204] Canon 488, 2°.

[205] Schaefer, *op. cit.,* n. 44.

[206] Lega-Bartoccetti, *op. cit.,* I, 139, n. 5; Schaefer, *op. cit.,* n. 394; Coronata, *Institutiones,* III, n. 1119; Roberti, *De Processibus,* I, 211; Wernz-Vidal, *op. cit.,* VI, n. 93.

[207] Canon 1579, § 2. Cf. Schaefer, *op. cit.,* n. 161.

§ 2, 2°.[208] The writer subscribes to this opinion for the following reason. According to canon 1558 all judges other than those who are mentioned for the cases listed under canons 1556 and 1557 would be absolutely incompetent.

In all other cases in which a controversy arises between corporations of different exempt clerical institutes or monastic congregations the court of first instance is that of the local ordinary.[209]

3) *Cases between corporations of the same non-exempt or lay religious institute.* If a controversy arises between corporations of the same non-exempt religious institute or of the same lay religious community, this case must be heard in the first instance before the local ordinary.[210] The clause of canon 1579, § 3, which declares this procedural principle uses the word "religious," but there seems to be no doubt that the moral person is also comprehended by the term.[211] Included as one of the lay institutes herein mentioned is an institute of nuns (*moniales*), even though it would be exempt in other matters, and were subject to a religious order of men.[212]

4) *Actions between corporations of religious institutes and secular clerics, lay persons, or lay moral persons (non-religious, but erected by ecclesiastical authority).* In a controversy between a corporation and a secular cleric, a lay person, or a lay corporation erected by ecclesiastical authority, the local ordinary is the judge in the first instance. This, of course, is not a religious tribunal or court of first instance.[213] But, if the corporations involved have no superior below the Roman Pontiff, then these corporations would follow the prescripts of canon 1557, § 2, 2°.[214] The clause of canon 1579, § 3, here discussed, likewise uses the word "religious," but there seem to be very obvious and necessary reasons for including under this term the moral person composed of religious.[215]

---

[208] Beste, *Introductio in Codicem,* p. 768; Coronata, *Institutiones,* III, n. 1119.

[209] Canon 1579, § 3.

[210] Canon 1579, § 3.

[211] Lega-Bartoccetti, *Commentarius,* I, 139, n. 7; Roberti, *De Processibus,* I, n. 73, p. 210.

[212] Roberti, *op. cit.,* I, n. 73, p. 210.

[213] Canon 1579, § 3.

[214] Cf. Canon 1558.

[215] Lega-Bartoccetti, *Commentarius,* I, 139, n. 7.

CHAPTER VI

The Corporate Representation in the Contentious Trial

Article 1. Procedural Capacity

Juridic capacity, the title of Article 2 of Chapter V, is not the same in meaning as procedural capacity, the title of this Article. By virtue of his juridic capacity a person can be a party in a trial. The personal procedural capacity is that by which the person himself can place procedural acts in a trial. While juridic capacity constitutes the basis for procedural capacity, the latter is not a necessary consequence of the former.[1]

Procedural capacity is sometimes described as the *legitimatio ad processum.*[2] That is, as the intrinsic quality prerequisite in a litigant who intends to act personally in a trial.

Canon 1649 declares that the rights of moral persons, which are in law equal to minors,[3] are defended by their proper rector or administrator, except in the special cases mentioned in canon 1653; but, if there should exist a conflict of rights, canon 1649 requires the ordinary to appoint a procurator to represent the moral person. Since by its very nature the ecclesiastical corporation is incapable of performing procedural acts,[4] it is necessary that physical or natural persons initiate the suit of the corporation or respond to the suit against the corporation.[5] Thus canon 1649 states the general rule in designating for moral persons a lawful person to

---

[1] Eichmann, *Das Prozessrecht des Codex Iuris Canonici* (Paderborn, 1921), p. 89, § 2 (hereafter cited as *Das Prozessrecht*); Wernz-Vidal, *Ius Canonicum,* VI, n. 203, p. 171.

[2] Wernz-Vidal, *op. cit.,* n. 203, note 16; Roberti, *De Processibus,* I, n. 158, p. 465.

[3] Canon 100, § 3.

[4] Wernz-Vidal, *op. cit.,* VI, n. 209, p. 177; Vermeersch-Creusen, *Epitome,* III, n. 77.

[5] Roberti, *De Processibus,* I, n. 203.

represent them in a trial.[6] The prescripts of canon 1653 must be observed for the licit exercise of this faculty.[7]

But under the general rule mentioned in canon 1649—exception being properly made for the cases mentioned in canon 1653—is it necessary for the rector and the administrator to have the consent of the members of a collegiate moral entity to represent it in court? Obviously, if the rector and the administrator are delegated by a general mandate of the members of the corporation, which could include the power to act in administrative affairs and in trials, or by a special mandate with power to act in a particular affair or a special trial, the person so delegated could act in court for the moral person. Under such circumstances the permission is duly expressed, and any further manifestation of consent would be unnecessary.[8] If, then, from the expressed mandate, general or particular, the rector or administrator are designated to represent the moral person for trials, no further consent or permission seems to be called for.

But—again in abstraction from the cases mentioned in canon 1653—would the mere designation of an individual as the rector or as the ordinary administrator include the power to represent the collegiate entity without the consent of the members of that body? Noval (1861-1938) contended that a rector of a collegiate moral person would need the consent of the members according to the special requirement enacted in canon 1653. But he held that an administrator of a collegiate moral person would not need the consent of the members.[9] He regarded the power to represent the moral person in trials to be included in the power of ordinary administration.[10]

Roberti, on the other hand, holds[11] that the physical persons who represent the moral entity with only the ordinary power of administration would not be able to represent the legal person in

[6] Lega-Bartoccetti, *Commentarius,* I, 307, n. 7.

[7] Lega-Bartoccetti, *loc. cit.*

[8] Cf. Lega-Bartoccetti, *Commentarius,* I, 307, n. 7.

[9] Noval, *De Iudiciis,* n. 254. Cf. canon 1526 in reference to the initiating of a lawsuit in the name of a church by the administrator.

[10] Noval, *De Iudiciis,* n. 261.

[11] *De Processibus,* I, n. 203.

trial without the express permission of those on whom they depended for their appointment or delegation. Roberti argues that, since the acts of alienation are not within the scope of the power of the one deputed with the ordinary administration of affairs, an express permission is required for such an agent of the corporate entity to act in court for it, inasmuch as an unsuccessful defense could well entail an act of alienation in such an amount that its negotiation would lie outside the sphere of the administrator's power and authority.[12]

The writer is of the opinion that the one appointed to act as the ordinary administrator does not have the power to initiate lawsuits and defend them for and on behalf of the corporation unless he has received the permission of the superior or of the members of the corporate group, at least for the lawfulness of such acts. The particular power to act in trials seems to involve an act of greater importance than those which are necessarily a part of the ordinary administration.[13] Therefore permission should be obtained in authorization of such procedural acts.[14]

---

[12] *Loc. cit.*

[13] Comyns, *Papal and Episcopal Administration of Church Property,* p. 3.

[14] Coronata, *Institutiones,* III, n. 1175. *American Law*: The court, in Bosworth v. Allen, 168 N. Y. 157, referring to the directors, stated: "While not technically trustees, for the title of the corporate property was in the corporation itself, they were charged with the duties and subject to the liabilities of trustees. Clothed with the power of controlling the property and managing the affairs of the corporation, without let or hindrance, as to third persons they were its agents, but as to the corporation, itself, equity holds them liable as trustees (2 Pomeroy's Equity Jurisprudence, secs. 1061, 1063, 1088, 1097)." Cf. People ex Rel. Manice v. Powell, 201 N. Y. 194, 94 N. E. 634. Directors must act as a board. Cf. Hoyle v. Plattsburgh & M. R. Co., 54 N. Y. 314, at p. 328, 13 Am. Rep. 595:—"Nor is it possible to limit the duty of a director of a corporation, in this respect, to the time while he is acting as director under any special delegation of power, or in attendance at meetings of the Board." Corinne Mill, Canal & Stock Co. v. Toponce, 152 U. S. 405, 38 L. Ed. 493, 14 Sup. Ct. 632, in which Brewer, J. said at p. 408: "No duty was cast on any individual director as such. The board of directors, as a body, were charged with the usual duty of care of the affairs of the corporation, but all the power and duty cast upon them was upon them as a board, and not individually. When a corporation in a given matter is empowered to act only through its board of directors, or other select body of

If the rights of the moral person conflict with those of the rector or the administrator, the ordinary shall designate a procurator[15] to represent it in court.[16] This procurator is considered as appointed or designated by the ordinary, in virtue of his administrative or extra-judicial power, before the trial begins. If the conflict arises or is revealed during the trial, then the judge in the trial appoints the procurator to represent the moral person.[17]

According to canon 1653, § 3,[18] prelates and the superiors of chapters, sodalities and other collegiate bodies or corporations cannot act in court in the name of their community or organization except with its consent according to its statutes.

Through its use of the term "prelates," the Code in canon 1653, § 3, points to clerics, either secular or religious, who have ordinary jurisdiction in the external forum.[19] The superiors of the chapters

---

its officials, individual or separate action of the members of such board is not sufficient. The agent of the corporation is the board itself acting in its organized capacity, and not its members acting independently of its meetings."—Monroe Mercantile Co. v. Arnold, 108 Ga. 449; Branch v. Augusta Glass Works, 95 Ga. 573; England v. Dearborn, 141 Mass. 590; Mitchell v. Rome R. Co., 17 Ga. 574.

[15] The procurator is the personal representative of a party litigant, and is properly named *procurator ad litem*. The designation of a procurator is a formal appointment which must be deposited with the court before procedural acts are undertaken. Cf. Woywod, *A Practical Commentary on the Code of Canon Law* (4. ed., 2 vols., New York: J. F. Wagner, 1932), II, 232. If the procurator acts in court with an invalid mandate, his invalid acts result in a null sentence. Cf. canon 1892, 3°.

The rules of the Sacred Roman Rota call for the presence of the promoter of justice in contentious trials involving moral persons. The promoter is described by the rules as the natural defender of the rights of moral persons, and in consequence he is to vindicate these rights everywhere. In the judicial forum the promoter is obliged to see that these entities are given the full protection of law. *Normae S.R.R. Tribunalis,* 29 iun. 1934, art. 27, 28—*AAS,* XXVI (1934), 457; Signatura Apostolica, *Tergestina, Recursus seu Proventus et Emolumentorum,* 15 mart. 1921—*AAS,* XIII (1921), 269-273.

[16] Canon 1649.

[17] Cf. canons 1648, §§ 2, 3; 1655, § 2; Lega-Bartoccetti, *Commentarius,* I, 307, n. 6.

[18] This writer will not discuss paragraphs one and two of canon 1653 because they deal directly with non-collegiate bodies.

[19] Cf. Canon 110.

herein referred to are the immediate superiors, for example, the Deans. The chapters here referred to are secular ones.[20] The superiors of sodalities and other corporations, as referred to in the canon under discussion, are either the rectors or the administrators of these moral collegiate entities.[21]

Prelates and superiors cannot appear, then, in the name of the chapter, of the sodality or any other collegiate body, without the consent of the community as prescribed by its statutes.[22] The statutes here referred to are based on the franchise or the certificate of incorporation, or on the decree of erection issued by the competent ordinary.

Lay persons can represent a collegiate moral person, such as a confraternity, if these persons are members of the corporation according to its statutes.[23] The bishop who presides over a community is not dispensed by law from obtaining the permission of the community for initiating a suit or defending a suit of the moral person.[24]

Some canonists interpret the clause of canon 1653, § 3, namely, *"sine eiusdem consensu ad normam statutorum,"* as meaning that the consent is always required unless the statutes provide otherwise.[25] Other canonists maintain that the consent of the corporation is not required unless the statutes expressly provide for it.[26]

---

[20] Noval, *De Iudiciis,* n. 258, p. 162.

[21] Noval, *op. cit.*

[22] Canon 1653, § 3.

[23] Roberti, *De Processibus,* I, n. 204, p. 561.

[24] Roberti, *loc. cit.*

[25] ". . . ita ut hic [consensus] intelligendus sit quidem praescriptus, sed nisi statuta aliud habeant. Aliunde vero, si statuta aliud non habeant, consensum communitatis exquirere debent administratores. . . ."—Noval, *De Iudiciis,* n. 258, p. 163. "Possunt tamen statuta necessitatem consensus excludere; quod si non faciant, vi huius canonis consensus est necessarius."—Coronata, *Institutiones,* III, n. 1175, p. 82. "Sed possunt statuta decernere consensum . . . in certis casibus nullo modo requiri."—Vermeersch-Creusen, *Epitome,* III, n. 78. Lega-Bartoccetti (*Commentarius,* I, 324) seems to hold this opinion also.

[26] "Cum autem lex rem ex statutis definiat, consensus non requiritur nisi statuta requirant."—Roberti, *De Processibus,* I, n. 204, p. 561. ". . . at sine consensu suae communitatis, nisi statuta aliud habeant."—De Meester, n. 1558, p. 36. Augustine (*A Commentary,* VII, 104) based his opinion on the distinction used by the pre-Code authors on this question, although he

This latter seems the better opinion, for in the preliminary drafts of the Code there was a clause which stated that the consent of the community was required unless the statutes provided otherwise, but this was omitted in the final draft and hence does not appear in the Code.[27]

Some canonists hold that the consent of the corporate body would not be necessary for the validity of the trial, provided that the statutes required it merely for licitness.[28] Noval held[29] that the representative designated for a trial in such cases would act validly under such circumstances, but he based his opinion on the supposition that such representative action fell within the power of ordinary administration. Roberti holds[30] the contrary opinion, on the grounds that the consent referred to in canon 1653, § 3, is required for the validity of the trials and is of the essence of the right to represent the moral person, inasmuch as the law decrees nullity for the trial in the absence of such a given consent. This seems to be the better opinion on this matter, and it certainly is the more common one among the canonists.[31]

---

admitted that in America there is no distinction between the *mensa abbatis* and the *mensa communitatis*. In other words, Augustine's opinion is based on the supposition that the statutes of a community distinguish between the property or revenues proper to the prelate or superior, or at least subject to his own personal administration, and the goods which this person administers in the name of the community. In the latter case Augustine required the consent of the community, according to the statutes of the community; in the former case he did not require the community's consent. But Augustine admitted that in a religious community wherein the members take solemn vows this distinction would have little weight, except in orders where the *peculium* still existed.

[27] ". . . stare in iudicio nequeunt, nomine respectivae communitatis, absque eius consensu, salvis constitutionibus et statutis particularibus legitime recognitis quae aliud caveant."—Roberti, *Codicis Iuris Canonici Schemata,* Lib. IV, *De Processibus* (Typis Polyglottis Vaticanis, 1940), Schema G, c. 113, § 3; F. c. 115, § 1; D. c. 130, § 1; C. c. 105, § 1.

[28] Coronata, *Institutiones,* III, n. 1174, p. 82, note 4; Vermeersch-Creusen, *Epitome,* III, n. 78.

[29] *De Iudiciis,* I, n. 259.

[30] *De Processibus,* I, n. 204, p. 561.

[31] Couly, "Les Parties en Cause—Personnes Morales Religieuses, Excommuniées"—*Le Canoniste,* XLVIII (1926), 386; Eichmann, *Das Prozessrecht,* p. 92; Lega-Bartoccetti. *Commentarius,* I, 324, n. 5.

This conclusion is confirmed by the fact that the permission is of the essence of the power or right to represent the moral person in the trial.[32] Furthermore, when the Code requires consent only for the lawfulness, and not for the validity of an action, it notes this fact explicitly.[33] Besides, the invalidating force does not stem from the particular constitutions or statutes of the ecclesiastical corporation, but from the law of the Code.[34] The statutes can determine whether or not consent is required, but once they have determined that it is required, then failure to obtain it on the part of the representative would, in virtue of canons 105, 1°, and 1653, § 3, render the trial null.

When the administrator of a corporation is also required to obtain the permission of the ordinary in order to sue or to defend a suit entered against the corporation,[35] the consent of the community or of the collegiate body does not release the administrator from the necessity of obtaining the consent of the ordinary. While this permission of the ordinary ought to be in writing, this is not necessary for its validity. Without this permission, however, the acts are invalid, and the community is not responsible for the outcome of the suit,[36] since the representation before the court exceeds, in this case at least, the limits of ordinary administration.[37]

Both the consent of the community and the ordinary's permission when required by law ought to be obtained before the trial begins, that is, before the exhibition of the complaint or at least before the joinder of issue. Once the required permission and consent have been obtained, they are sufficient for an authorized performance of all procedural acts, including the taking of oaths and the making of confessions, but they are not sufficient for the renunciation of the action or suit.[38]

If the prelate or the superior has acted in a trial without due consent or permission, then the community or the collegiate body

---

[32] Cf. canons 105, 1°; 1892, 2°.

[33] Cf. canon 1653, §§ 1, 2.

[34] Roberti, *De Processibus,* I, n. 204, p. 561; cf. canon 105, 1°.

[35] Canon 1526.

[36] Canon 1527, § 1.

[37] Cf. *supra,* pp. 204-206.

[38] Roberti, *De Processibus,* I, n. 204, p. 562. Cf. canon 1653, § 6.

has the right to an action for damages against him.[39] If there is present in these cases a deliberate will on the part of the prelate, superior or other representative to violate the law,[40] criminal action, if such lies, can be taken against him and, in connection with it, the tort action arising therefrom can be tried by the criminal court.[41] Indemnification may not be sought by means of the judicial action of *restitutio in integrum.*[42] This action is one given by law to compensate for damages arising from any transaction by a rescission of the whole transaction. However, an invalid act cannot be attacked by means of this action, since the act does not exist in the eyes of the law and therefore, cannot be rescinded. Only valid, but rescindible, acts can be the basis of this remedy.[43]

The local ordinary may either in person or through another act in court for the moral persons under his jurisdiction whenever the administrator of such persons fails to defend or is negligent in the defense of its rights.[44] The administrator may fail to appear in view of such reasons as the previous fact of his death, his affliction with illness or the factor of hardship which makes it of great inconvenience for him to represent the moral person in court. The failure to appear may, on the other hand, arise from some moral impossibility, such as sheer inertia or the lack of skill in the management of affairs.[45] Negligence may also be the cause of the failure to sue or answer in a suit entered against the moral person, and this negligence may arise from the failure to observe and comply with the provisions of canon 1523 regarding the obligations of administrators.

The local ordinary can institute or defend a suit for the protection of the rights of any moral person within his jurisdiction when-

---

[39] Canon 1653, § 4.

[40] Canon 2200.

[41] Canon 2210, § 2.

[42] Cf. Canon 1687, § 1.

[43] Feeney, *Restitutio in Integrum,* The Catholic University of America Canon Law Studies, n. 129 (Washington, D. C.: The Catholic University of America Press, 1941), p. 69.

[44] Canon 1653, § 5.

[45] Lega-Bartoccetti, *Commentarius,* I, 325, n. 7; Noval, *De Iudiciis,* n. 260, p. 164; Roberti, *De Processibus,* I, n. 206, p. 572.

ever the proper administrator is under restraint and guilty of negligence in this matter. There seems to be no question among the canonists that the local ordinary, as the supervisory administrator of ecclesiastical goods in his territory and under his jurisdiction,[46] may bring an action, or defend one, as a public act on his part to protect and safeguard the rights and property committed to his care.[47]

Now the question arises: Under canon 1653, § 5, in which capacity does the local ordinary stand in court for the moral person? Is the local ordinary standing in trial in his own proper capacity as supervisory administrator of the ecclesiastical goods under his jurisdiction, but belonging to a particular moral person? Or is he merely an extraordinary administrator designated by canon 1653, § 5, to act for and in behalf of the moral person when its ordinary administrator is negligent or under restraint?

Coronata holds[48] that within the confines which canon 1653, § 5, indicates for the local ordinary, he may act in either capacity, that is, in his own proper capacity as supervisory administrator or also in his devolved capacity as extraordinary administrator.

Lega-Bartoccetti hold[49] that under the same circumstances the local ordinary acts as an extraordinary administrator in the name of the moral person. This view is primarily based on the words used in the Code, namely, *"in iudicio nomine personae moralis,"* as indicating an extraordinary administrator. The writer is of the same opinion for the same reason.

Roberti, on the contrary, holds[50] that the local ordinary in the case under discussion would act in such trials in his public capacity for the protection of the ecclesiastical goods of the moral person under his jurisdiction.

In practice, in the opinion of this writer, the local ordinary should by decree declare his intention of acting for a particular moral person under and in accordance with the provisions of canon 1653,

---

[46] Canon 1519.

[47] Lega-Bartoccetti, *Commentarius,* I, 326, n. 7; Coronata, *Institutiones,* I, n. 1175, p. 83; Roberti, *De Processibus,* I, n. 206, p. 572.

[48] *Institutiones,* III, n. 1175, p. 83.

[49] *Commentarius,* I, 326, n. 7.

[50] *De Processibus,* I, n. 206, pp. 571-572.

§ 5, thus excluding the possible action of the ordinary administrator in the trial. In this decree the local ordinary could also state in which capacity he intends to act. Or the matter of the capacity and intention to act could be raised by means of a judicial exception. But even without a decree, and though no judicial exception has been raised, the local ordinary stands in court for the beneficiary, and there can be no question of nullity concerning such a trial on the score of any doubtful capacity on the part of the local ordinary.[51]

The local ordinary may delegate another person, such as the promoter of justice,[52] to initiate a suit or defend one in the event that the ordinary administrator is under restraint or is guilty of negligence as postulated in canon 1653, § 5.

Religious superiors can, but only according to their constitutions or the statutes of their communities, represent in trials the religious collegiate moral person subject to them.[53] The superiors here referred to are not precisely prelates who have ordinary jurisdiction in the external forum as defined in canon 501. Rather, these superiors include those persons who as members of men and women religious institutes, or of particular houses and provinces of the latter,[54] enjoy the particular power to safeguard the rights of the corporations and to administer its temporalities.[55]

While the invalid actions of a representative for a corporation in court will, in general, entail an irremedial nullity for the process, and hence also for the sentence or the decision,[56] this eventuality may be obviated by means of a subsequent ratification of the preceding invalid acts, unless the adverse party takes an exception to the capacity for this action, or unless the court *ex officio* rules against it in an action initiated within thirty years of the publica-

---

[51] Cf. Lega-Bartoccetti, *Commentarius,* I, 326, n. 7.

[52] Roberti, *De Processibus,* I, n. 206, 572.

[53] Canon 1653, § 6.

[54] Canons 531; 532, 536; 1667.

[55] Noval, *De Iudiciis,* n. 261; Coronata, *Institutiones,* III, n. 1175, p. 82; Lega-Bartoccetti, *Commentarius,* I, 326, n. 8; Augustine, *A Commentary,* VII, 104.

[56] Canon 1892, 2°.

tion of the sentence, or at any time[57] during any period of the trial.[58]

ARTICLE 2. THE JUDICIAL ADVOCATES AND PROCEDURES FOR CORPORATIONS

In the preceding Article a treatment was offered, in accordance with canons 1649 and 1653, of the obligation in virtue of which an ecclesiastical corporation is required to act in court through a representative who has some antecedent bond of union with the moral person. The present Article will deal with the corporation's right to procedural representation through persons not otherwise associated with it, namely, by means of representation through advocates and procurators *ad litem.*

Canon 1655, § 2, declares in part that in contentious trials which involve minors the judge shall *ex officio* assign an advocate to an unrepresented defendant or, if necessary, add another advocate to the one chosen by the party.

According to the common opinion of canonists, the collegiate moral person is contemplated under canon 1655, § 2, since it is under the law regarded as a minor.[59]

The term advocate or lawyer signifies a qualified person who is entitled under the law to practice before the duly constituted courts.[60]

The party to a suit can also, according to canon 1655, § 3, freely appoint an advocate or procurator to plead or defend the case for him. A procurator *ad litem* is a commissioned agent appointed by a principal to act in court for him.[61]

The general rule of law implicitly contained in canon 1655, § 3, is that one may do those things through another which one himself

---

[57] Canon 1893.

[58] Roberti, *De Processibus,* I, n. 204, p. 564.

[59] Blat, *Commentarium,* Lib. IV, 159; Noval, *De Iudiciis,* n. 271. Cf. canon 100, § 3.

[60] Woywod, *A Practical Commentary on the Code of Canon Law,* II, n. 1629.

[61] Woywod, *op. cit.,* II, n. 1629.

is capable of doing.[62] According to this principle of law a procurator *ad litem* may be empowered by a corporation, or one delegated by it with a general mandate, to act in court for it.[63]

Religious can act as procurators in cases in which the good of their own institute is concerned, in accordance with their own constitutions and with the permission of their superiors.[64]

When a person is commissioned to act as procurator for a corporation in court, the mandate should be very clear in its terms of delegation of this person. If the mandate is illegal for any reason, the sentence in the trial will be irremediably null.[65] The procurator, of course, must act within the scope of his employment. The principal will not be bound by the acts of the procurator which exceed the limits of his power as defined in the mandate.[66] If the procurator, while acting within the defined limits of his mandate, will perpetrate a fraud or act negligently in any way, the principal will be bound to the consequences as regards third parties. The principal may, however, seek redress from the procurator for such injury.[67]

The mandate must be in writing in order to have a valid effect.[68] If this written mandate concedes full and complete power to the procurator, then this agent may perform all necessary acts for that person in court, except those acts for which a special mandate is required by law or which would prejudice the rights of the principal. For example, the procurator could not renounce judicial acts, waive judgment by default, effect a compromise or settlement, or arbitrate the issues involved.[69] But under a general mandate the

---

[62] Reg. 68, R.J., in VI°: "Potest quis per alium, quod potest facere per seipsum."

[63] Cf. Hogan, *Judicial Advocates and Procurators,* The Catholic University of America Canon Law Studies, n. 133 (Washington, D. C.: The Catholic University of America Press, 1941), p. 73.

[64] Canon 1657, § 3.

[65] Canon 1892, 3°.

[66] Canon 203, § 1.

[67] Coronata, *Institutiones,* III, n. 1191; Lega-Bartoccetti, *Commentarius,* I, 347.

[68] Cf. Hogan, *Judicial Advocates and Procurators,* p. 106.

[69] Cf. canons 1316, § 2; 1662; 1746. Canonists seem to be in disagreement on the question whether in these special cases, a special mandate is required for validity or merely for lawfulness. Cf. Hogan, *op. cit.,* pp. 115-116.

procurator may take an appeal in the case, unless the contrary appears in his commission.[70]

The procurator may be dismissed by the principal at any stage of the trial. The principal must give due notice to the procurator, and the removal becomes effective when this notice is received. If the procurator is removed after issue has been joined, the judge and the adverse party must likewise receive notice of the dismissal, in order that it may take effect.[71]

ARTICLE 3. THE TRIAL IN WHICH CORPORATIONS ARE PARTIES

The scope of this dissertation treats of the corporation in contentious and criminal trials insofar as these legal entities follow judicial procedural rules which differ from those pertaining to the ordinary party litigants. In the present Article the treatment of the contentious trial involving corporations will be limited to those particular and peculiar procedural rules which are applicable to these moral persons. In other phases of the trial, the corporation proceeds in the same manner, through its representative, as any other party plaintiff or defendant.

Summons. The summons should properly contain the full name of the incorporated body, or the name of its administrator or duly constituted representative, with due indication of this representative's capacity, so that no mistake will be made as to the true party in litigation.[72]

The summons must be communicated by messenger, mail or edict, to those individuals who are, according to canons 1649 and 1653, determined by law as endowed with the capacity to answer in court for the corporation.[73]

Canon 1723 indicates the need of carefully fulfilling all the necessary details prescribed by canon 1715 for the issuing of the summons when it declares that a summons which does not conform to legal norms is null, and thereby the subsequent procedural acts are null and void.

---

[70] Canon 1664, § 2.

[71] Canon 1664, § 1.

[72] S.R.R., *Treviren,* 15 maii 1913—*AAS,* V (1913), 285.

[73] Cf. canon 1713.

Procedural Acts. The representatives of the corporation, as determined under the rules of canons 1649 and 1653, may perform all procedural acts, including the taking of oaths and the making of a confession, but they do not have the power of renouncing the action.[74]

Procedural representatives other than those mentioned in canon 1649 and 1653 may, if they have a general mandate, perform all necessary acts for the corporation in whose interest they stand in court, with the exception of renouncing the suit, or its judicial acts, of waiving judgment by default, or of effecting a settlement of the case by compromise or arbitration.[75] Representatives with a special mandate must observe the terms of their mandate. In the trial they may execute all, but also only those, acts which were authorized by the mandate.[76]

---

[74] Roberti, *De Processibus,* I, n. 204, p. 562.

[75] Cf. canons 1316, § 2; 1662; 1746.

[76] Hogan, *Judicial Advocates and Procurators,* pp. 115-116.

CHAPTER VII

The Corporation in the Criminal Trial

ARTICLE 1. VICARIOUS IMPUTATION OF CORPORATE GUILT

The controversy whether a moral person is capable of a canonical delict and subject to a canonical penalty,[1] has its solution certainly in the very disposition of the laws by which such penalties were enacted in pre-Code law[2] and are now enacted in the law of the Code.[3] In the Code's adherence to the view recognizing corporate delictual responsibility, evident from the penal sanctions it declares for the criminal acts of the juristic person, there seems to be ample proof of a consistent legal doctrine. For, if the juristic person is capable of rights and obligations in law then there is no inconsistency in holding that in relation to the use of these rights

[1] Chelodi, *Ius Canonicum de Delictus et Poenis et de Iudiciis Criminalibus* (5. ed., recognita et aucta a Pio Ciprotti, Vicenza: Società Anonima Tipografica, 1943), n. 5, p. 6 (hereafter cited *De Delictis.*); Coronata, *Institutiones,* IV, n. 1642; Eichmann, *Lehrbuch des Kirchenrechts* (4. ed., 2 vols., Paderborn, 1934), II, § 290; Regatillo, *Institutiones Iuris Canonici,* II, n. 873; Roberti, *De Delictis,* n. 72; Wernz-Vidal, *Ius Canonicum,* VII, n. 37 (II).

[2] C. 23, X, *de electione et electi potestate,* I, 6; c. 40, X, *de electione et electi potestate,* I, 6, in VI°; Conc. Trident., sess. VII, *de ref.,* c. 10; Conc. Trident., sess. XXIII, *de ref.,* c. 10; Lega, *De Delictis et Poenis* (2. ed., Romae, 1910), nn. 50, 68; Wernz, *Ius Decretalium,* VI, 24.

[3] Canons 2255, § 2; 2274, § 1; 2285, § 1; 2291, 1°; 2332; 2391, § 1. Cf. Chelodi, *op. cit.,* n. 5, p. 6; Coronata, *op. cit.,* IV, n. 1642; D'Annibale, *Summula Theologiae Moralis* (3 vols., Romae, 1888-1892), I, 44; Gillet, *La Personalité Juridique,* p. 258; Regatillo, *Institutiones Iuris Canonici,* II, n. 873; Augustine, *A Commentary,* VIII, 12; Ayrinhac-Lydon, *Penal Legislation in the New Code of Canon Law* (rev. ed., New York: Benziger Brothers, 1936), n. 108, p. 83 (hereafter cited *Penal Legislation*). For the contrary opinion, cf. Roberti, *op. cit.,* I, n. 73, p. 102. There he writes: "*Censemus* sanctiones aliquando etiam iure canonico in personas morales irrogatas et origine historica et bono publico explicari. Verius videtur proprie dicta imputabilitas poenalis personis moralibus applicari non posse."

and the fulfillment of these obligations as established in law the corporation can commit a crime or canonical delict.[4]

However, it is necessary, for the imposition of a canonical penalty, that the corporation itself be responsible for the crime or delict attributed to it. This fact will be verified, generally, if the collegiate juristic person proceeds in the accomplishment of a criminal act by or with the consent of the absolute majority of

---

[4] Coronata, *Institutiones,* IV, n. 1642; Gierke, *Genossenschaftsrecht,* III, 234. *American Law*: It was the opinion of the earlier writers on common law that a corporation could not commit a crime. It is said to have been held by Lord Chief Justice Holt (Anonymous, 12 Modern, 559) that "a corporation is not indictable, although the particular members of it are." In Blackstone's *Commentaries,* Ch. 18, § 12, it is stated: "A corporation cannot commit treason, or felony, or other crime in its corporate capacity, though its members may in their distinct individual capacities."

Modern authorities incline the other way. Generally, both in the state and in federal jurisdictions, a corporation is subject to punishment for its criminal acts. Mr. Chief Justice Field stated in Telegram Newspaper Company v. Commonwealth, 172 Mass. 294: "We think that a corporation may be liable criminally for certain offenses of which a specific intent may be a necessary element. There is no more difficulty in imputing to a corporation a specific intent in criminal proceedings than in civil. A corporation cannot be arrested and imprisoned in either civil or criminal proceedings, but its property may be taken either as compensation for a private wrong or as punishment for a public wrong." The corporation was held for criminal contempt.

In the federal jurisdiction, a leading case is New York Central and Hudson River Railroad Co. v. United States (1908), 212 U. S. 481, 53 L. Ed. 613, 29 Sup. Ct. 304, in which the court imputed the act of an agent to his employer and imposed penalties upon the corporation.

It is now well established that in actions for tort the corporation may be held responsible for damages for the acts of its agents within the scope of their employment.—Lake Shore & Michigan Southern R. R. v. Prentice, 147 U. S. 101, 109, 111.

It is true that there are some crimes which in their nature cannot be committed by corporations. In People v. Rochester Ry. & Light Co., 195 N. Y., 102, the court said: "A definition of certain forms of manslaughter might be formulated which would be applicable to corporations" (p. 107). Under the New York Penal Code, sec. 179, however, which defines homicide as "the killing of one human being by the act, procurement or omission of another," meaning another human being, it was held that a corporation could not be guilty of this crime. Cf. also United States v. New York Herald Co., 159 Fed. 296; Canfield, "Corporate Responsibility for Crime,"—14 *Columbia Law Review* 469.

those members who enjoy the privilege of voting according to law.[5]

Once the imputability of guilt for corporate delicts or crimes is established in the law, the consideration of the extension of this imputability becomes of paramount importance. It may be said that the collegiate moral person is subject to punishment, either in a criminal action or by the enforcement of legal redress in a contentious action, when it has committed a delict or crime,[6] or has attempted to commit a crime[7] which is imputable to it, according to the measure of its legal nature and capacity.[8]

In like manner it must be granted that the canonical penalties inflicted for delicts imputed to the ecclesiastical corporation as such ought to be in accordance with its nature which is peculiar to itself. These penalties are principally the withdrawal or suspension of the rights which the moral person itself is entitled otherwise to exercise,[9] and the imposition of fines and forfeitures.[10] On the other hand, the direct imposition of the penalty of excommunication is absolutely impossible.[11]

ARTICLE 2. THE CANONICAL PENALTIES FOR CORPORATE DELICTS

There are three kinds of censures[12] in ecclesiastical penal law: excommunication, interdict and suspension.[13] Since the censure of

---

[5] Cf. canon 101, § 1; Coronata, *Institutiones,* IV, n. 1642, p. 11; Regatillo, *Institutiones Iuris Canonici,* II, n. 873.

[6] Canon 2195. This canon defines a crime, in ecclesiastical law, as an external and morally imputable transgression of a law to which is attached a canonical sanction, of at least an indefinite character.

[7] Cf. canon 2212.

[8] Cf. Coronata, *Institutiones,* IV, n. 1642, p. 10; Regatillo, *Institutiones Iuris Canonici,* II, n. 873; Wernz-Vidal, *Ius Canonicum,* IV, n. 37, p. 52 (II).

[9] Chelodi, *De Delictis,* n. 5; Hollweck, *Die kirchliche Strafgesetze* (Mainz, 1899), § 11, note 2.

[10] Coronata, *Institutiones,* IV, n. 1642, p. 11.

[11] Canon 2255; c. 5, X, *de sententia excommunicationis,* V, 11, in VI°; Ayrinhac-Lydon, *Penal Legislation,* n. 108; Augustine, *A Commentary,* VIII, 164; Regatillo, *Institutiones Iuris Canonici,* II, n. 985; Cappello, *Summa Iuris Canonici* (Vols. I-II, 4. ed., 1945; Vol. III, 2. ed., 1940, Romae: Apud Aedes Universitatis Gregorianae), III, n. 508, p. 460.

[12] A canonical censure is defined by canon 2241, § 1, as a penalty by which a baptized person, delinquent and contumacious, is deprived of certain spiritual goods or goods connected with spiritual ones, until he has given up his contumacy and is absolved.

[13] Canon 2255, § 1.

excommunication can affect only natural or physical persons, the application of a penalty of excommunication to a collegiate moral person, while valid according to canon 2255, § 2,[14] is to be interpreted as affecting the individual members of the corporate body in so far as such members participated or shared in the crime or delict.[15]

Suspension[16] and interdict[17] as canonical penal sanctions can be inflicted on a collegiate moral person, for example, on a college, a university, or a chapter.[18] According to canon 2286, vindinctive penalties are those which are directly intended for the expiation of offenses, and hence their remission does not depend on the mere cessation of contumacy. The primary purpose of this type of penalty is to avenge the public order.[19] Suspension and interdict may be imposed for a definite or fixed period of time. When so imposed these penalties are vindictive rather than medicinal or

---

[14] Ayrinhac-Lydon, *Penal Legislation*, n. 108; Cf. Cappello, *De Censuris* (3. ed., Taurinorum Augustae: Marietti, 1933), n. 139, 11°; Regatillo, *Institutiones Iuris Canonici*, II, n. 985. Wernz-Vidal maintain (*Ius Canonicum*, VII, n. 274) that the censure of excommunication can never be promulgated ("*numquam promulgari potest*") against a university, a college or a community as a community, but only directly against determined individuals. They seem to hold that the application itself to the moral person would be invalid. Blat certainly holds (*Commentarium*, Lib. V, n. 80, p. 122) that such an application would be invalid.

[15] Blat, *Commentarium*, V, n. 80, p. 122; Cappello, *De Censuris*, n. 139, 11°; Chelodi, *De Delictis*, n. 36; Regatillo, *Institutiones Iuris Canonici*, II, n. 985; Wernz-Vidal, *Ius Canonicum*, VII, n. 274, p. 283; Augustine, *A Commentary*, VIII, 164; Ayrinhac-Lydon, *Penal Legislation*, n. 108, p. 83.

[16] Canon 2278, § 1, defines a canonical suspension as a censure by which a cleric is forbidden to exercise the rights of his office, of his benefice, or of both.

[17] Canon 2268 declares that an interdict is a censure by which the faithful, remaining in communion with the Church, are deprived of certain spiritual rights. The canon further states that this deprivation of spiritual rights is effected either directly by means of a personal interdict, or indirectly by means of a local interdict.

[18] Canons 2255, § 2; 2274, § 1; 2285, § 1.

[19] Cf. Conran, *The Interdict*, The Catholic University of America Canon Law Studies, n. 56 (Washington, D. C.: The Catholic University of America, 1930), p. 2.

corrective penalties.[20] The medicinal penalties have for their primary purpose the correction of the wrongdoer, and for their secondary purpose the prevention of crime on the part of other offenders.

The individual members of the juristic person, although innocent, are bound to respect the censures of interdict and suspension, when and if imposed on the corporate body, but only as members of the body, not as individuals. Consequently a member would cease to be bound as soon as he ceases to be a member of the corporation. He would likewise not be bound as an individual, even while he continues to be a member of the corporation, if he has not been the cause of the interdict. Accordingly, if he is not forbidden by reason of any other censure, he may receive the sacraments, even apart from any absolution from the interdict and apart from any act of previous satisfaction.[21]

The general personal interdict,[22] which is the canonical penalty inflicted on a number of persons forming a corporate body, affects the corporation itself and the members as a part thereof, as long as they maintain their membership in the corporation. The infliction of this penalty presupposes some corporate fault or guilt, namely, the commission of some delinquency by a community or a college, as a body, and the penalty itself is of a personal nature, following the juristic person everywhere.[23] The penalty suspends the exercise of spiritual rights which the corporation may legally possess, such as, e.g., the right of election,[24] of presentation, and of nomination of candidates for office.[25]

An interdict may be imposed on a collegiate moral body forever, or for a specified period of time, or for as long as the superior in his discretion determines.[26]

Universities, colleges, chapters or other moral persons, by whatsoever name they may be known, incur an interdict reserved in a

---

[20] Arynhac-Lydon, *Penal Legislation*, n. 76, p. 58.

[21] Canons 2255, § 2; 2276; Aryinhac-Lydon, *Penal Legislation*, n. 108, p. 83.

[22] Canon 2274, § 1.

[23] Cappello, *De Censuris*, n. 466; Chelodi, *De Delictis*, n. 39.

[24] Blat, *Commentarium*, Lib. V, n. 102, p. 154; Cappello, *De Censuris*, n. 466 (2).

[25] Cappello, *loc. cit.;* Augustine, *A Commentary*, VIII, 211.

[26] Canon 2291, 1°.

special manner to the Apostolic See, if an appeal is made by them from the laws, decrees or mandates of the reigning Roman Pontiff to an Oecumenical Council.[27]

Suspension may be incurred by a collegiate body of clerics in the same way and on the same conditions as the penalty of interdict.[28] The corporate body under a penalty of suspension would be denied the exercise of such rights that would be proper to it as a corporate body of clerics.[29]

Even though there be no specific penalty attached to the violation of a given law, the legitimate superior nevertheless may, even without the previous threat of any penalty, punish the transgression with some just penalty, if the scandal given or the special gravity of the violation demands it.[30]

ARTICLE 3. THE CRIMINAL PROCEDURAL ACTION AGAINST THE CORPORATION

It is not within the scope of this dissertation to treat of the general rules of criminal procedure. Its scope relates to only those rules which may apply in a special way to moral persons. It may be stated, however, that there do not appear to be set forth in the Code any rules of criminal procedure which have special application to the ecclesiastical corporation as such.

In the accusation, the hearing and the conclusion, a criminal trial involving an ecclesiastical corporation follows those rules which are applicable to other persons in general. Special note, however, should be made of canon 1959. This canon insists that, with regard to the elements of procedure in criminal cases not mentioned in canons 1933 to 1959, the rules stated in the First Part (on trials in general) of the Fourth Book are to be followed, and that in the application of penalties the law of the Fifth Book must be observed.

---

[27] Canon 2332.

[28] Canon 2285, § 1.

[29] Regatillo, *Institutiones Iuris Canonici*, II, n. 1025.

[30] Canon 2222, § 1.

The ordinary may entrust to the promoter of justice or to a procurator the prosecution of a trial for damages arising out of a delict.[31] But the same judge who tries the criminal action can at the instance of the injured party try and decide the civil action.[32]

---

[31] Glynn, *The Promoter of Justice,* The Catholic University of America Canon Law Studies, n. 101 (Washington, D. C.: The Catholic University of America, 1936), p. 205.

[32] Canon 2210, § 2. This canon employs the word "civil" in contradistinction to the word "criminal." It is evident, then, that a contentious suit is involved when there is question simply of the recovery of damages.

CONCLUSIONS

1. Legal recognition of the corporate entity's juridic right, as an attribute of its autonomy, to prosecute and to defend its claims in court was early established in Roman Law (p. 21), and was adopted and followed by ecclesiastical jurisprudence both in pre-Code (p. 29) and in Code law (p. 59).

2. The corporation's unfettered growth gave rise to the formulation of a stable procedural method for the juristic person. This of necessity required representation by physical persons for the execution of its procedural acts. In Roman Law this representative was usually designated by the term *syndicus* (p. 21) and this same term was taken over by Church law (p. 41). *Syndicus* remained the proper designation for the trial representative of ecclesiastical moral persons until a later pre-Code period, when it was supplanted by the term *procurator,* as now in use under the Code (p. 9). However, the terms *syndicus* and *procurator,* as used in Canon Law, usually pointed, and under the Code still point, to the extraordinary trial representative.

3. The ordinary trial representative for corporations in Canon Law, not only in pre-Code legislation but also in the legislation of the Code, is usually the superior of the corporate body. In pre-Code law the right of the superior of a corporation to institute a suit or to respond to one in defense of the corporate rights apart from the consent of the corporate body represented by him was in dispute. As a general rule, the more common opinion acknowledged the right to the superior to execute the procedural acts apart from the consent of the corporate membership (pp. 32-33). But, if the administration of goods was reserved in a special way to the corporate membership, or if there was a joint administration of goods by the superior and the body, or if the matter in question was of an arduous nature, the consent of the community was always required (p. 33). Under the Code, provided that nothing to the contrary is mentioned in the statutes, the one appointed to act as ordinary administrator does not have the power to institute law-

suits and defend them for and on behalf of the corporation, unless he has received the permission of the superior or of the members of the corporate group, at least for the lawfulness of such acts (p. 100). When by the statutes of a corporation the consent is required for the corporate officer to prosecute and vindicate the corporate rights in court, that consent, according to the Code, is of the essence of his right to represent the corporation, so that without this consent his procedural acts will be null and void (p. 103).

4. The ancient heritage of the corporate entity's substantive rights in Roman Law was acknowledged by the Church. All substantive rights granted to the corporation and recognized by both the Roman Law and the pre-Code ecclesiastical law were rights consonant with the nature of the moral person recognized by law. While the Roman Law did not extend the capacity of the moral person to the point of acknowledging its capacity to commit a crime (p. 25), it did permit legal redress against the corporation for its civil torts (p. 25). The imputation of crime to a corporation was admitted by Canon Law in the pre-Code period, but the extent of the corporation's capacity to commit crimes was in dispute (p. 36). The Code legislation adopted the legal principle of the corporate capacity to commit certain crimes, and accordingly it has enacted penalties for such corporate wrongdoing (p. 112). In both the pre-Code and in the legislation of the Code the corporation is responsible for damages caused by its tortious acts (pp. 40, 114).

5. A corporation may initiate a proprietary action for the declaration of its legal status as a corporation (p. 57).

6. The ecclesiastical moral person does not enjoy the privilege of the forum (*privilegium fori*) (p. 67).

7. The reservation of competence declared by canon 1557, § 2, 1°, does not include the contentious cases of residential bishops if they represent collegiate moral persons under their jurisdiction (p. 76).

8. The corporation which enjoys the exclusive and reserved competence of the Sacred Roman Rota under canon 1557, § 2, 2°, is entitled to it whether the moral person is party plaintiff or party defendant (p. 77).

9. Whether the corporation is plaintiff or defendant in a suit in which the other party is either the administrator, the beneficiary, or

a member, and the cause concerns an act of administration, the proper place for the trial is before the local ordinary of the place where the act of administration in question was placed. If the other party to the case is a third party or a stranger to the corporation, the ordinary rules of competence must be observed, even though the case concerns an act of administration (p. 89).

10. The ecclesiastical corporation has a juridical seat, residence or domicile for the purposes of canon 1561, § 1, in the place where it was constituted or erected (p. 91).

BIBLIOGRAPHY

Sources

Acta Apostolica Sedis, Commentarium Officiale, Romae, 1909-.

Acta Sanctae Sedis, 41 vols., Romae, 1865-1908.

Bruns, H. Th., *Canones Apostolorum et Conciliorum Saeculorum IV-VII,* 2 vols., Berolini, Reimeri, 1839.

Bullarii Romani Continuatio Summorum Pontificum, 19 vols., Prati, 1756-1883.

Bullarum Diplomatum et Privilegiorum Sanctorum Pontificum Taurinensis Editio, 24 vols. et Appendix, Augustae Taurinorum, 1857-1872.

Codex Iuris Canonici Pii X Pontificis Maximi iussu digestus Benedicti Papae XV auctoritate promulgatus, Romae, 1917.

Codicis Iuris Canonici Fontes, cura Emi Petri Card. Gasparri Editi, 9 vols., Romae (postea Civitate Vaticana): Typis Polyglottis, 1923-1939 (Vols. VII-IX, ed. cura et studio Emi Iustiniani Card. Serédi).

Corpus Iuris Canonici, editio Lipsiensis secunda post Aemilii Ludovici Richteri curas ad librorum manu scriptorum et editionis Romanae fidem recognovit et adnotatione critica instruxit Aemilius Friedberg, Lipsiae, 1879-1881.

Corpus Iuris Civilis, Vol. I, *Institutiones,* ed. stereotypa 15.—recognovit P. Krueger; Vol. I, *Digesta,* ed. stereotypa 15.—recognovit T. Mommsen, retractavit P. Krueger; Vol. II, *Codex Iustinianus,* ed. stereoptypa 10.—recognovit et retractavit P. Krueger; Vol. III, *Novellae Constitutiones,* ed. stereoptypa 5.—R. Schoell; opus Schoellii morte interceptum absolvit G. Kroll, Berolini: apud Weidmannos, 1928-1929.

———, *Digesta Iustiniani Augusti*—recognoverunt et ediderunt P. Bonfante, C. Fadda, C. Ferrini, S. Riccobono, V. Scialoia, Mediolani: Società Editrice Libraria, 1931.

Decretales D. Gregorii Papae IX, una cum Glossis Restitutae, Romae, 1582.

Decretum Gratiani Emendatum et Notationibus Illustratum una cum Glosis, Romae, 1582.

Jaffé, Philippus, *Regesta Pontificum Romanorum ab condita ecclesia ad annum post Christum natum MCXCVIII,* 2 ed., correctam et auctam auspiciis Gulielmi Wattenbach, curaverunt S. Loewenfeld, F. Kaltenbrunner, P. Ewald, 2 vols. in 1, Lipsiae, 1885-1888.

Potthast, Augustus, *Regesta Pontificum Romanorum inde ab A. post Christum natum MCXCVIII ad A. MCCCIV,* 2 vols., Berolini, 1874-1875.

Raccolta di Concordati su Materia Ecclesiastiche tra la Santa Sede e le Auctorità Civili (1098-1914), ed. A. Mercati, Roma: Tipografia Poliglotta Vaticana, 1919.

Sacrae Romanae Rotae Decisiones seu Sententia (ab anno 1909), Romae: Typis Vaticanis, 1912-.

Schroeder, H. J., *Canons and Decrees of the Council of Trent,* St. Louis: B. Herder & Co., 1941.

REFERENCE WORKS

Anderson, Walter, *Limitations of the Corporate Entity,* St. Louis, Mo.: Thomas Law Book Company, 1931.

Attwater, Donald, *A Catholic Dictionary,* New York: The Macmillan Co., 1941.

Ayrinhac, H. A., *General Legislation in the New Code of Canon Law,* New York, 1923.

———, - Lydon, P. J., *Penal Legislation in the New Code of Canon Law,* revised edition, New York: Benziger Bros., 1936.

Augustine, Charles, *Rights and Duties of Ordinaries,* St. Louis, Mo.: B. Herder & Co., 1924.

———, *A Commentary on the New Code of Canon Law,* 8 vols., St. Louis, Mo.: B. Herder & Co., 1925-1938. Vol. I, 6. ed., 1931; Vol. II, 6. ed., 1936; Vol. III, 5. ed., 1938; Vol. IV, 3. ed., 1925; Vol. V, 5. ed., 1935; Vol. VI, 3. ed., 1931; Vol. VII, 3. ed., 1930; Vol. VIII, 3. ed., 1931.

Barbosa, Augustinus, *Pastoralis Sollicitudinis sive de Officio et Potestate Episcopi Tripartita Descriptio,* Lugduni, 1656.

———, *Collectanea Doctorum tam Veterum quam Recentiorum in Jus Pontificum Universum,* 2 vols., Lugduni, 1716.

Bernardus Papiensis, *Summa Decretalium,* ed. E.A.T., Laspeyres, Ratisbonae, 1860.

Beste, Udalricus, *Introductio In Codicem,* 2. ed., Collegeville, Minn.: St. John's Abbey Press, 1944.

Blackstone, W., *Commentaries on the Law,* ed. B. C. Gavit, Washington: Washington Law Book Co., 1941.

Blat, Albertus, *Commentarium Textus Codicis Iuris Canonici,* 5 vols. in 7. Romae: Ex Typographia Pontificia in Instituto Pii IX, 1921-1938. Lib. I, 1921; Lib. II, pars I, editio altera, 1921; Lib. II, partes II, III, ed. tertia, 1938; Lib. III, partes I, III, 2. ed. aucta et emendata, 1924; Lib. III, partes IV-VI, 2. ed. examinata denuo et aucta, 1934; Lib. IV, 1927; Lib. V, 1924.

Bouix, D., *Tractatus de Judiciis Ecclesiasticis,* 2. ed., 2 vols., Parisiis, 1855.

Bouscaren, T. L., *The Canon Law Digest,* 2 vols., Milwaukee: Bruce, 1934-1943.

Bouvier, J., *Law Dictionary,* 3. rev. ed., 2 vols., St. Paul, Minn.: West Publishing Co., 1914.

Brown, Brendan, *The Canonical Juristic Personality with Special Reference to its Status in the United States of America,* The Catholic University of America Canon Law Studies, n. 39, Washington, D. C.: The Catholic University of America, 1927.

Buckland, W. W., *Elementary Principles of Roman Private Law,* Cambridge: University Press, 1912.

———, *A Text-Book of Roman Law from Augustus to Justinian,* 2. ed., Cambridge: University Press, 1932.

———, *A Manual of Roman Private Law,* 2. ed., Cambridge: University Press, 1939.

Canfield, G.,-Wormser, I. M., *Cases on Private Corporations,* 2. ed., Indianapolis: The Bobbs-Merrill Co., 1925.

Cappello, Felix, *Institutiones Iuris Publici Ecclesiastici,* 2 vols., Taurinorum Augustae, 1907-1908.

———, *Summa Iuris Publici Ecclesiastici,* Romae, 1923.

———, *De Censuris,* 3. ed., Taurinorum Augustae: Marietti, 1933.

———, *Summa Iuris Canonici,* Vol. I, editio quarta accurate recognita, 1945; Vol. II, editio quarta accurata recognita et aucta, 1945; Vol. III, editio altera emendata et aucta, 1940, Romae: Apud Aedes Universitatis Gregorianae.

Carmody, Francis, *A Treatise on New York Practice,* revised by Edward Carr, New York: Clark Boardman Co., Ltd., 1931.

Carter, James, *The Nature of the Corporation as a Legal Entity,* Baltimore: Curlander, 1919.

Cavagnis, F., *Institutiones Iuris Publici Ecclesiastici,* 4. ed., 3 vols., Romae: 1906.

Chelodi, Ioannes, *Ius Canonicum de Personis,* 3. ed., curavit P. Ciprotti, Trento: Libreria Moderna Editrice, 1942.

———, *Ius Canonicum de Delictis et Poenis et de Iudiciis Criminalibus,* 5. ed., recognita et aucta a Pio Ciprotti, Vicenza: Società Anonima Tipografica, 1943.

Cicognani, Amleto, G., *Canon Law,* 2. rev. ed., Authorized English Version by J. M. O'Hara and F. Brennan, Philadelphia: Dolphin Press, 1935.

Cleary, Joseph, *Canonical Limitations on the Alienation of Church Property,* The Catholic University of America Canon Law Studies, n. 100, Washington, D. C.: The Catholic University of America, 1936.

Cocchi, Guidus, *Commentarium in Codicem Iuris Canonici,* 8 vols. in 5, 1920-1930, Vol. VII, *De Processibus,* 3. ed., 1940, Taurinorum Augustae, Marietti.

Colquhoun, Patrick, *Roman Civil Law,* 3 vols., London: Benning, 1849.

Comyns, Joseph, *Papal and Episcopal Administration of Church Property,* The Catholic University of America Canon Law Studies, n. 147, Washington, D. C.: The Catholic University of America Press, 1942.

Conran, Edward, *The Interdict,* The Catholic University of America Canon Law Studies, n. 56, Washington, D. C.: The Catholic University of America, 1930.

Coronata, Matthaeus Conte a, *Institutiones Iuris Canonici,* 5 vols., Romae: Marietti, Vols. I-IV editio altera aucta et emendata, Vols. I-II, 1939; Vol. III, 1941; Vol. IV, 1945; Vol. V, 1936.

Corporation Manual, 1946, New York: United States Corporation Co.

Costello, John, *Domicile and Quasi-Domicile,* The Catholic University of America Canon Law Studies, n. 60, Washington, D. C.: The Catholic University of America, 1930.

Coyle, Paul, *Judicial Exceptions,* The Catholic University of America Canon Law Studies, n. 193, Washington, D. C.: The Catholic University of America Press, 1944.

D'Annibale, J., *Summula Theologiae Moralis,* 3. ed., Romae, 1888-1892.

De Meester, Alphonsus, *Juris Canonici et Juris Canonico-Civilis Compendium,* nova editio, 3 vols. in 4, Brugis: Desclée De Brouwer, 1921-1928.

Dernburg, Heinrich von, *System des römischen Rechts,* 2 vols., Berlin, 1912.

Doheny, W. J., *Practical Problems in Church Finance,* Milwaukee: The Bruce Publishing Co., 1941.

Downs, John, *The Concept of Clerical Immunity,* The Catholic University of America Canon Law Studies, n. 126, Washington, D. C.: The Catholic University of America Press, 1941.

Durandus, Gulielmus, *Speculum Iuris,* 3 vols., Venetiis, 1577.

Eichmann, Eduard, *Das Prozessrecht des Codex Iuris Canonici,* Paderborn, 1921.

———, *Lehrbuch des Kirchenrechts,* 4. ed., 2 vols., Paderborn, 1934.

Fagnanus, Prosper, *Commentaria in Quinque Libros Decretalium,* 4 vols., Romae, 1661.

Fanfani, Ludovicus, *De Iure Religiosorum,* Taurini-Romae: Marietti, 1920.

Feeney, Thos., *Restitutio in Integrum,* The Catholic University of America Canon Law Studies, n. 129, Washington, D. C.: The Catholic University of America Press, 1941.

Ferraris, Lucius, *Prompta Bibliotheca Canonica, Iuridica, Moralis, Theologica, necnon Ascetica, Polemica, Rubricistica, Historica,* 9 vols., Romae, 1885-1899.

Gierke, Otto, *Das deutsche Genossenschaftsrecht,* 4 vols., Berlin: Weidmannsche Buchhlandlung, 1881-1913.

———, *Political Theories of the Middle Ages,* translated with an introduction by Maitland, Cambridge: University Press, 1922.

Gillet, Pierre, *La Personalité Juridique en Droit Ecclésiastique,* Universitas Catholica Lovaniensis, Malines: W. Godène, 1927.

Girard, Paul F., *Manuel Elémentaire de Droit Romain,* 7. ed., Paris: Rousseau, 1924.

Glynn, John, *The Promoter of Justice,* The Catholic University of America Canon Law Studies, n. 101, Washington, D. C.: The Catholic University of America, 1936.

Gonzalez-Tellez, Emmanuel, *Commentaria Perpetua in singulos textus quinque librorum Decretalium Gregorii IX,* 5 vols., 1699.

Haskins, Charles Homer, *Norman Institutions,* Cambridge: Harvard University Press, 1925.

Heylen, V., *De Iure et Iustitia,* 4. ed., 2 vols., Mechliniae: H. Dessain, 1943.

Hicks, Frederick, *Materials and Methods of Legal Research,* 3. rev. ed., Rochester, N. Y.: Lawyers Co-operative Company, 1942.

Hogan, James, *Judicial Advocates and Procurators,* The Catholic University of America Canon Law Studies, n. 133, Washington, D. C.: The Catholic University of America Press, 1941.

Hohenlohe, Constantine, *Papstrecht und weltliches Recht,* München, 1925.

Holdsworth, William S., *A History of English Law,* 3. ed., 9 vols., London: Methuen, 1923.

Hollweck, Joseph, *Die kirchlichen Strafgesetze,* Mainz, 1899.

Holmes, Oliver Wendell, Jr., *The Common Law,* Boston: Little, Brown & Company, 1943.

Hostiensis (Henricus de Segusio), *Summa Aurea,* Basileae: 1573.

Innocentius IV (Sinibaldus Fliscus), *Apparatus in Libros Quinque Decretalium,* Venetiis: 1481.

Ioannes Andreae, *In Quinque Decretalium Libros Novella Commentaria,* 4 vols., Venetiis: 1581.

Jenks, Edward, *Law and Politics in the Middle Ages,* New York: Holt & Co., 1898.

———, *The Book of English Law,* Boston: Houghton, Mifflin Co., 1929.

———, *A Short Outline of English Legal History,* 4. ed., London: Sweet & Maxwell, 1945.

Jolowicz, H. F. *Historical Introduction to the Study of Roman Law,* Cambridge: University Press, 1932.

Klekotka, P., *Diocesan Consultors,* The Catholic University of America Canon Law Studies, n. 8, Washington, D. C.: The Catholic University of America, 1920.

Król, John J., *The Defendant in Contentious Trials,* The Catholic University of America Canon Law Studies, n. 146, Washington, D. C.: The Catholic University of America Press, 1942.

LeBuffe, F.,-Hayes, James, *Jurisprudence,* 3. rev. ed., New York: Fordham University Press, 1938.

Lega, M. Card., *De Delictis et Poenis,* 2. ed., Romae, 1910.

———,-Bartoccetti, V., *Commentarius in Iudicia Ecclesiastica iuxta Codicem Iuris Canonici,* 3 vols., Romae: Anonima Libraria Cattolica Italiana, 1938-1941.

Maitland, Frederick, *Domesday Book and Beyond,* Cambridge, London: University Press, 1897.

Maroto, Philippus, *Institutiones Iuris Canonici,* 2 vols., Matriti, 1918-1919.

Michiels, P. Gommarus, *Principia Generalia de Personis in Ecclesia,* Lublin: Universitas Catholica, 1932.

———, *De Delictis et Poenis,* Lublin: Universitas Catholica, 1934.

Morawetz, Victor, *A Treatise on the Law of Private Corporations,* 2. ed., Boston: Brown, Little, Brown, 1886.

Muñiz, T., *Procédimientos Eclésiasticos,* 2. ed., 3 vols., Seville: Lib. de Sobrino de Izquierdo, 1926.

Neuberger, Nicholas, *Canon 6,* The Catholic University of America Canon Law Studies, n. 44, Washington, D. C.: The Catholic University of America, 1927.

Noval, J., *Commentarium Codicis Iuris Canonici,* Lib. IV, *De Processibus,* Pars I, *De Iudiciis,* Augustae Taurinorum: Marietti, 1920.

Ottaviani, Alaphridus, *Institutiones Iuris Publici Ecclesiastici,* 2. ed., 2 vols., Civitate Vaticana: Typis Polyglottis, 1935-1936.

Panormitanus (Nicholas de Tudeschis), *Commentaria in Quinque Libros Decretalium,* 5 vols. in 7, Venetiis, 1588.

Pejška, Joseph, *Ius Canonicum Religiosorum,* 3. ed., Friburgi-Brisoviae: B. Herder Book Co., 1927.

Philostratus, *Vitae Sophistarum,* English translation by Wright, Loeb Classical Library.

Pirhing, E., *Jus Canonicum in Quinque Libros Decretalium Distributum,* 5 vols., Dilingae, 1674-1678.

Pistocchi, Marius, *De Bonis Ecclesiae Temporalibus,* Taurini: Marietti, 1932.

Pollock, F.,-Maitland, F. W., *A History of English Law,* 2. ed., 2 vols., Cambridge: University Press, 1923.

Reeves, John,-Finlason, W. F., *History of the English Law,* 5 vols., Philadelphia: Murphy, 1880.

Regatillo, E., *Institutiones Iuris Canonici,* 2 vols., Santander: Sal Terrae, 1941-1942.

Reiffenstuel, Anacletus, *Jus Canonicum Universum,* 5 vols. in 7, Parisiis, 1864-1870.

Roberti, Franciscus, *De Delictis et Poenis,* Romae: Apud Aedes Facultatis Iuridicae ad S. Apollinaris, 1 vol. in 2, 1930-1938.

———, *Codicis Iuris Canonici Schemata,* Lib. IV, *De Processibus,* Romae: Typis Polyglottis Vaticanis, 1940.

———, *De Processibus,* Vol. I, 2. ed., Romae: Apud Custodiam Librariam Pontificii Instituti Utriusque Iuris, 1941.

Salmond, John, *Jurisprudence,* 7. ed., London: Sweet & Maxwell, 1924.

Schaefer, Timotheus, *De Religiosis ad Normam Codicis Canonici,* 3. ed., Romae: S.A.L.E.R., 1940.

Schmalzgrueber, F., *Ius Canonicum Universum,* 5 vols. in 12, Romae, 1843-1845.

Schmier, Franciscus, *Iurisprudentia Canonico-Civilis,* 2 vols., Venetiis, 1754.

Schnorr von Carolsfeld, Ludwig, *Geschichte der juristischen Person,* Vol. I, München: Beck, 1933.

Sherman, C. P., *Roman Law in the Modern World,* 2. ed., 3 vols., New York: Baker Voorhis & Co., 1927.

Sipos, Stepnaus, *Enchiridion Iuris Canonici,* 3. ed., Pécs: Ex Typographia "Haladás, R. T.," 1936.

Smith, William, *Dictionary of Greek and Roman Antiquities,* 2 vols., London, 1890.

Sohm, Rudolph, *The Institutes of Roman Law,* translated by James Crawford Ledlie, 3. ed., Oxford, 1926.

Stubbs, William, *Lectures on Medieval and Modern History,* 3. ed., Oxford, 1900.

Tarquini, Camillus, *Institutiones Iuris Publici Ecclesiastici,* 4. ed., Romae, 1865.

Taylor, Henry O., *A Treatise on the Law of Private Corporations,* Philadelphia, 1884.

Van Hove, A., *Commentarium Lovaniense in Codicem Iuris Canonici,* Vol. I, Tom. I, *Prolegomena ad Codicem Iuris Canonici,* 2. ed., Mechliniae-Romae: H. Dessain, 1945.

Vermeersch, Arthurus-Creusen, Josephus, *Epitome Iuris Canonici,* 4. ed., 3 vols., Mechliniae-Romae: H. Dessain, 1929-1931.

Vromant, G., *De Bonis Ecclesiae Temporalibus,* 2. ed., Louvain: Museum Lessianum, 1934.

Webster, Noah,-Merriam, A., *New International Dictionary,* 2. ed., Springfield, Mass.: G. & C. Merriam Co., 1942.

Wenger, L., *Institutes of the Roman Law of Civil Procedure,* translated by Otto Fisk, rev. ed., New York: Veritas Press, 1940.

Wernz, Franciscus, *Ius Decretalium,* 2. ed., 6 vols., Romae et Prati, 1906-1913.

———,-Vidal, Petrus, *Ius Canonicum,* 7 vols. in 9, Romae: Universitas Gregoriana, 1927-1946, Vol. I, 1938; Vol. II, 3. ed., a P. Philippo Aguirre recognita, 1943; Vol. III, 1933; Vol. IV, Pars I, 1934; Vol. IV, Pars II, 1935; Vol. V, 3. ed., a P. Philippo Aguirre recognita, 1946; Vol. VI, 1927; Vol. VI, Pars altera, 1928; Vol. VII, 1937.

Wormser, I, Maurice, *Disregard of the Corporate Fiction and Allied Corporation Problems,* New York: Baker, Voorhis & Co., 1929.

Woywod, Stanislaus, *A Practical Commentary on the Code of Canon Law,* 4. ed., 2 vols., New York: J. F. Wagner, 1932.

Articles

Anonymous, "The Juridical Status of the Parishes of Religious"—*The Jurist,* I (1941), 329-335.

Canfield, George, "Corporate Responsibility for Crime"—14 *Columbia Law Review,* 469.

Ciprotti, Pius, "De Privilegio Fori quoad Personas Iuridicas"—*Antonianum,* XII (1937), 165-170.

Couly, A., "Les Biens Temporals de l'Eglise"—*Le Canoniste Contemporain,* XLV (1922), 305-320, 395-405.

———, "Les Parties en Cause-Personnes Morales, Religieuses, Excommuniées"—*Le Canoniste,* XLVIII (1926), 381-291.

Gierke, Otto, "Juristische Person"—*Rechtlslexikon,* by Holtzendorff, Leipzig, 1875, n. 943, 844-849.

Hannan, Jerome, "Parochial Ownership"—*The Homiletic and Pastoral Review,* XLII (1941), 255-267.

Larraona, Arcadius, "Commentarium Codicis"—*CpR*, III (1922), 45-53.

Laski, Harold, "The Early History of the Corporation in England"—30 *Harvard Law Review*, 561-588.

Laurin, F., "Wesen und Bedeutung des Domizils"—*Archiv für katholisches Kirchenrecht*, XXVI (1871), pp. 165-249, § 10.

Lenel, Otto, "E. Albertario, 'Syndicus' *BIDR*"—*Zeitschrift der Savigny-Stiftung für Rechtsgeschichte*, Romanistische Abteilung, XLIV (1924), 550.

Machen, Arthur W. Jr., "Corporate Personality"—24 *Harvard Law Review*, 253-267.

Post, Gaines, "*Plena Potestas* and Consent in Mediaeval Assemblies"—*Traditio*, I (1943), 355 ff.

———, "Roman Law and Early Representation in Spain and Italy, 1150-1250"—*Speculum*, XVIII (1943), 211-232.

Pollock, F., "Has the Common Law Received the Fiction Theory of Corporations?"—27 *The Law Quarterly Review*, 219-235.

Roberti, F., "De Privilegio Fori"—*Apollinaris*, III (1930), 635-637.

Vindex, "Domicilium et Quasi-Domicilium"—*Jus Pontificum*, VI (1926), n. 33, p. 44 and n. 52, p. 53.

Zollman, Carl, "Classes of American Religious Corporations"—13 *Michigan Law Review*, 566.

———, "Nature of American Religious Corporations"—14 *Michigan Law Review*, 37.

Periodicals

Antonianum, Romae, 1926-.

Apollinaris, Romae, 1928-.

Archiv für katholisches Kirchenrecht, Innsbruck, 1857-1861; Mainz, 1862-.

Commentarium pro Religiosis, Romae, 1920-; ab anno 1935, *Commentarium pro Religiosis et Missionariis*.

Columbia Law Review, New York, 1901-.

Homiletic and Pastoral Review, The, New York, 1900-.

Harvard Law Review, Cambridge, Mass., 1887-.

Jurist, The, Washington, 1941-.

Jus Pontificum, Romae, 1921-.

Le Canoniste Contemporaine, Paris, 1878-1922; ab anno 1924-1926, *Le Canoniste*.

Law Quarterly Review, The, London, 1885-.

Michigan Law Review (University of Michigan), 1902-.

Speculum, A Journal of Mediaeval Studies, The Medieval Academy of America, Cambridge, Mass., 1926-.

Traditio, New York, 1943-.

Zeitschrift der Savigny-Stiftung für Rechtsgeschichte, Roman. Abtlg., Weimar, 1880-.

Abbreviations

AAS—Acta Apostolicae Sedis.
A.L.R.—American Law Reports, Annotated.
Am. Rep.—American Reports (selected Cases), Albany.
App. Div.—New York Supreme Court, Appellate Division Reports.
ASS—Acta Sanctae Sedis.
Ass.—Liber Assissarum or Pleas of the Crown (Book of Assizes), Pt. 5 of Year Books.
Barb.—Barbour, Supreme Court Reports, New York, 67 vols.
Black—Black, U. S. Supreme Court Reports, vols. 66-67.
C.—Codex Iustinianus.
CpR—Commentarium pro Religiosis.
Cranch—United States Supreme Court Reports, Vols. 5-13.
D.—Digest.
Ed.—Edward.
Fed.—The Federal Reporter, United States.
Fontes—Codicis Iuris Canonici Fontes cura . . . Gasparri editi.
Ga.—Georgia; Georgia Reports.
Hil.—Hilary Term.
Hun.—New York Supreme Court Reports, 92 vols.
Hy.—Henry.
How.—Howard, United States Supreme Court Reports, Vols. 42-65.
Ill.—Illinois; Illinois Reports.
Jaffé—*Regesta Pontificum Romanorum ad annum MCXCVIII* (edited by Ewald, Kaltenbrunner, Löwenfeld).
L.Ed.—Lawyers' Edition, United States Supreme Court Report.
L.R.A.—Lawyers' Reports, Annotated (New York).
Mass.—Massachusetts; Massachusetts Reports.
Mich.—Michaelmas Term.
Misc.—Miscellaneous Reports, New York.
Mo.—Missouri; Missouri Reports.
Modern—Modern Reports, English King's Bench, etc., 12 vols.
N.E.—Northeastern Reporter, National Reporter System.
N.W.—Northwestern Reporter.
N.Y.—New York; New York Court of Appeals Reports.
N.Y.Supp.—New York Supplement Reports, National Reporter System.
Pa.—Pennsylvania; Pennsylvania Reports.
Pasch.—Paschal or Easter Term.
Potthast—*Regesta Pontificum Romanorum ab anno MCXCVIII ad annum MCCCIV.*
S.C. de Sem. et Univ. Stud.—Sacra Congregatio de Seminariis et Universitatibus Studiorum.
Sup. Ct.—Supreme Court Reporter, National Reporter System.

Trin.—Trinity Term.
U.S.—United States; United States Reports.
Wheat.—Wheaton's United States Supreme Court Reports, Vols. 14-25.
Wisc.—Wisconsin; Wisconsin Reports.
Y.B.—Year Books, English King's Bench, etc., cited by year of King's reign.

TABLE OF AMERICAN CASES CITED

PAGE

Alexander Canal Co. v. Swann, 5 How. 83, 12 L.Ed. 60 60
Austin v. Telephone Co., 73 Hun. 96, 25 N. Y. Supp. 916 93
Baltimore & R. R. Co. v. Fifth Baptist Church, 137 U. S. 568, 34 L.Ed. 784, 11 Sup. Ct. 185 60
Bank of United States v. Deveaux, 5 Cranch (U. S.) 61 93
Bartlett v. Lily Dale Assembly, 139 Misc. 338, 249 N. Y. Supp. 482 58
Baxter v. McDermott, 155 N. Y. 83 71
Bosworth v. Allen, 168 N. Y. 157 100
Branch v. Augusta Glass Works, 95 Ga. 573 100
Calkins v. Cheney, 92 Ill. 463 71
City of St. Louis v. Ferry Co., 40 Mo. 580 93
Corinne Mill, Canal & Stock Co. v. Toponce, 152 U. S. 405, 38 L.Ed. 493, 14 Sup. Ct. 632 100
Dartmouth College v. Woodward, 4 Wheat. 518 70
England v. Dearborn, 141 Mass. 590 100
Galveston &c. R. Co. v. Gonzales, 151 U. S. 496, 38 L.Ed. 248 93
General Baking Co. v. Daniell, 181 A.D. 501, 170 N. Y. Supp. 365 93
Gram v. Prussia Emigrated Evangelical Lutheran German Society, 36 N. Y. 161 81
Hightower v. Thornton, 8 Ga. 486 70
Hoyle v. Plattsburgh & M. R. Co., 54 N. Y. 314, 13 Am. Rep. 595 100
Lake Shore & Michigan Southern R. R. v. Prentice, 147 U. S. 101 113
Levey v. Payne, 200 A.D. 30, 192 N. Y. Supp. 346 93
Merrick v. Van Santvoord, 34 N. Y. 208 93
Mitchell v. Rome R. Co., 17 Ga. 574 100
Monroe Mercantile Co. v. Arnold, 108 Ga. 449 100
New York Central & Hudson River Railroad Co. v. United States, 212 U. S. 481, 53 L.Ed. 613 113
North & South Rolling Stock Co. v. People, 147 Ill. 234, 35 N.E. 608, 24 L.R.A. 462 93
Ohio &c. R. Co. v. Wheeler, 1 Black (U. S.) 286, 17 L.Ed. 130 93
People v. Keese, 27 Hun. 483 81
People ex Rel. Manice v. Powell, 201 N. Y. 194, 94 N.E. 634 100
People v. Rochester Ry. & Light Co., 195 N. Y. 102 113
Poland v. United Transaction Co., 88 A.D. 281, 85 N. Y. Supp. affd. in 77 N. Y. 557 93
Rector of St. James Church v. Huntington, 82 Hun. 125 71
Robertson v. Bullions, 11 N. Y. 243 .... 71, 81

TABLE OF AMERICAN CASES CITED (Continued)

	Page
State ex re LaFollette v. Dammann, 220 Wisc. 17, 264 N.W. 627	58
Sullivan & Sons Mfg. Co. v. Ideal Bldg. & Loan Assoc., 313 Pa. 407	58
Telegram Newspaper Co. v. Commonwealth, 172 Mass. 294	113
United States v. Mac Andrews & Forbes Co., 149 Fed. 823	5
United States v. New York Herald Co., 159 Fed. 296	5, 13
Waller v. Howell, 20 Misc. 236, 45 N. Y. Supp. 790	71
Watkins v. Wilcox, 4 Hun. 220, affd. in 66 N. Y. 654	81
Watson v. Jones, 13 Wall 679	71
Wyatt v. Benson, 23 Barb. 327	81
Westminster Presbyterian Church v. Presbytery, 142 App. Div. 855, 127 N. Y. Supp. 836	71

BIOGRAPHICAL NOTE

Thomas John Kilcullen was born November 10, 1910, in Newark, New Jersey, and there attended St. Patrick's Cathedral School. After graduating from Leonardo High School, Leonardo, New Jersey, in 1927, he matriculated for the Pre-Legal Course at Fordham University, New York City. Fordham University's School of Law conferred on him the degree of the Baccalaureate in Law in June, 1932, and he was duly admitted to practice law before the Courts of the State of New York. He was admitted to the Post-Graduate School of Law of St. John's Law School, Brooklyn, New York, and the degree of Master of Laws was conferred on him in 1935. After having pursued his studies for the priesthood at Mount Saint Mary's Seminary, Emmitsburg, Maryland, he was ordained to the Priesthood for the Diocese of Scranton on May 30, 1942. With the approval of his bishop he was permitted to accept an invitation to teach at Mount Saint Mary's College. He was admitted to the School of Canon Law at the Catholic University of America in 1944, and was given the degree of the Baccalaureate in Canon Law in May, 1945, and the degree of the Licentiate in Canon Law in June, 1946.

INDEX

Abbot, defined, 30.
procedural rights of, 9 sq., 30-32, 41, 50.
Acts, legal, of corporation, 86.
Action,
contentious, of religious corporation, 95-97.
criminal, against corporation, 117 sq.
Actions, concerning benefice, 80.
de spolio, 79.
of administration, 81-90.
of debt, 52.
of ecclesiastical corporations, 95.
of religious institutes, 97.
possessory, 57-58.
proprietary, 57-58.
tort, 59, 114.
Actio legis, 20.
Actor, 21-23.
Actor et reus, 10.
Acts, procedural, 111.
Acquisition of domicile, 90-91.
by moral person, 91-94.
Adjective law, 27.
Administration,
actions concerning, 81-90.
by chapters, 85.
by local ordinary, 84-85.
classification of, 83-84.
definition of, 82-83.
forum for, 82.
immediate, 84 sq.
Administrator, classification of, 86.
corporate representative, 61, 99, 100-101.
designated by statute, 86.
Advocate, defined, 108.
for corporation, 108.
Aggregate corporation, defined, 7.
Association, lay, administrator of, 86.

Beneficiary of corporation, 87.
Body, corporate,
recognition of, 15.
privilege of forum, 63-72.

Capacity, juridic, defined, 98.
juridical, 28.
personal procedural, 98.
to commit crime, 25.
Chapters, actions concerning administration of, 81-90.
administration of, 85.
procedural rights of, 34-35.
Cathedral chapters, 83 fn.
Church, a moral person, 5.
a perfect society, 14, 62-63.
judicial power of, 62.
recognition of, 19.
Civil law, 16, 47.
defined, 3.
Code, Justinian, 18.
Collegia, 16, 20.
Collegiate church, defined, 84 fn.
Collegiate moral person, in Roman law, 17.
right to sue, 60.
Common law, 48.
English, 13 sq.
Community, procedural rights of, 34.
same lay religious, suits between, 97.
Competence, determination of, 72.
distinguished, 72.
for moral persons, 76-77.
of necessary forum, 73.
of ordinary forum, 73.
phases of, 73.
reserved, 73, 76.
Confraternities, privileged forum for, 65.
Congregatio monastica, defined, 88.
Congregation, exempt religious, moderator of, 75.
Consent, of corporate body for trials, 102-105.
Constitution of religious corporate body, 80-81 fn.
Contentious actions of religious corporation, 95-97.
Contentious trial, defined, 55.
Corporation,
a citizen, 93 fn.
aggregate, 7.
beneficiary of, 87.
capacity to commit crime, 25, 112-114.
concept of, 70 fn.
ecclesiastical, actions of, 95.
ecclesiastical, distinguished, 71.
English, defined, 47.
execution against, 25.

declaration of juridical fact about, 57.
in common law, 8, 13 sq., 50 sq.
of religious institute, suits of, 97.
legal acts of, 86.
represented by administrator, 99-101.
by chapter, 102.
by lay persons, 102.
by prelate, 102.
by procurator, 11, 108-109.
by rector, 99-101.
by superior, 33.
by superioress, 33.
by syndic, 43.
representation in trial of, 21-24, 61, 108, 110.
responsibility for crime, 112-115.
right to sue, 8, 21, 59-61.
sealed contracts of, 51.
secular, defined, 4-5.
sole, 7.
Corporate body, recognition by state, 5, 17-19, 71 fn.
Corporate bodies, privilege of forum, 67.
Corporate status, declaration of, 57.
Crime, corporate capacity to commit, 25, 51, 112-114.
Criminal trial defined, 55-56.

Declaration of, corporate status, 57.
juridical fact, 57.
Defensor, 21-23.
De spolio, action of, 79.
Determination of competence, 72.
Digest of Justinian, 20.
Domicile, acquisition of, 90-91.
in American law, 93 fn.
of moral persons, 91-94.

Ecclesiastical corporation, actions of, 95.
distinguished, 71.
lay, 71.
religious, 71.
rights and obligations of, 61.
Ecclesiastical law, 1.
Ecclesiastical person, in possessory suit, 57.
in proprietary suit, 57.
English law, corporate responsibility for crimes in, 51.
corporation defined in, 47.
corporation in, 13, 47, 50.
procedural rights of corporation in, 50, 52.
Execution against corporation, 25.
Exercise of jurisdiction, 62-63.
Excommunication, penalty of, 37, 115.

Forum, competent, defined, 78.
for moral persons, 72.
for pious bequests and legacies, 90.
for administration, 82.
necessary, 73, 78-90.
ordinary, 73, 90-94.
privileged, Code legislation, 66 sq.
concerning moral persons, 63-66.
defined, 63.
for confraternities, 65.
for dioceses, 66.
pre-Code legislation, 64 sq.

Goods, ecclesiastical, defined, 82.

Holy See, a moral person, 5.

Immediate administration, 84 sq.
Interdict, of moral person, 40, 115-116.
Institutes, administrators of, 86.
different exempt clerical, suits between, 96.
of Justinian, 18.
same non-exempt religious, suits between, 97.

Judgment, declaratory, 58 fn.
Judicial oaths, 25, 111.
Judicial power of Church, 62.
Juridic capacity, defined, 98.
Juridical capacity, 28.
of monastery, 29.
Juridical fact, declaration of, 57.
Jurisdiction, defined, 62.
distinguished from competence, 72.
exercise of, 62-63.
of religious tribunals, 95.
Justinian, Code of, 18.
Digest of, 20.
Institutes of, 18.

Kinds of moral persons, 5, 18.

Law, adjective, 27.
civil, 3, 16, 47.
common, 4, 8, 48.
ecclesiastical, 1.
Roman, 3, 16, 47.
statutory, 4.
substantive, 27.
Lay associations, administrator of, 86.

Legal acts of corporation, 86.
Legitmatio ad processum, 98.
Local ordinary, administration by, 84-85.

Moderators of exempt religious congregations, 75.
Monasteries, autonomous, suits between, 96.
  suits between different, 96.
Monastery, juridical capacity of, 29.
Moral being, capacity of, 3.
  representative of, 3, 9-12, 21-24, 30-34, 41, 61, 108-110.
Moral person,
  administrator of, 87, 98 sq.
  collegiate, 6-7.
    administrator of, 87, 98 sq.
  capacity for delictual act of, 36-40, 112-114.
  competence for, 76-77.
  composition of, 6, 59.
  declaration of status, 59.
  distinguished, 71.
  domicile of, 91-94.
  interdict on, 40, 115-116.
  non-collegiate, 6-7.
  privilege forum for, 64 sq.
  purpose of, 6.
  recognition of, 5, 17-19, 71 fn.
  right to sue, 8, 21, 50, 59-61.
  suspension of, 40, 115-117.

Necessary forum, 73.
Norman Conquest, 48-49.

Oaths, judicial, 25, 111.
Object of trial, 56.
Orders, moderators of, 75.
Ordinary forum, 73.
Ordinary, local, administration by, 84-85.
  as corporate representative, 105-106.

Penalty, for corporate delicts, 40-41, 114-117.
Perfect society, church a, 14, 62-63.
Prelate, defined, 30.
  of seculars, 35.
  of religious, 35.
  procedural rights of, 30, 32, 34.
Person, juridical, 1.
  juristic, criminal acts of, 112-115.
  moral, 1.
    composition of, 6.
    criminal acts of, 112-115.
    criminal procedural action against, 117 sq.
    defined, 2.
    fiction theory of, 2.
    penalties against, 115-117.
    realist theory of, 2.
    recognition of, 5.
Personal procedural capacity, 81-90.
Phases of competence, 73.
Possessory suit, 56.
Privileged forum, see FORUM.
Procedural capacity, defined, 98.
Procedural rights, of chapters, 34-35.
  of community, 34, 97.
Procurator ad litem, 11, 108-109.
Procurator,
  dismissal of, 109.
  mandate of, 109.
  office of, 41, 45.
  who may act as, 109.
Property, corporate administration of, 87-88.
Proprietary suit, 57-58.
Power, judicial, of Church, 62.
Proceedings, formulary, 20.
Province, religious, defined, 95-96.
  nature of, 96.
Provinces, suits between, 96.

Quasi-domicile, corporate, 90-92.

Rector, corporate representation by, 61, 99-101.
Religious province, defined, 95-96.
Religious tribunals, jurisdiction of, 95.
Right to sue, corporate, 8, 21, 50, 59-61.
Rights and duties correlative, 1.
Rights and obligations, of ecclesiastical corporation, 61.
  of representative, 12, 30-34, 108-110.
Roman law, 3, 16, 47.
  collegiate moral person in, 17.
Representation, corporate, 21-24, 61, 108-110.
  by administrator, 61, 99, 100-101.
  by rector, 61.
Representation, procedural, notion of, 9-13.
  by abbot, 30-32, 41.
  by prelate, 30-32, 34.
  by superior, 33.
  by superioress, 33.

Representative, rights and duties of, 12, 30-34, 108-110.
Reserved competence, 73, 76.
Responsibility, delictual, of corporation, 112-115.
Restitutio in integrum, 26, 46, 51, 54.
Reus et actor, 10.
Rota, Sacred Roman, 74.
  reserved competence of, 77.

Sealed contracts of corporation, 51.
Secular corporation, defined, 4-5.
Society, a perfect, 14.
  the Church as, 62-63.
Societies, religious, administrators of, 66.
Sodalitates, 16.
Sole, corporation, 7.
Spiritual censures, 40.
State, a perfect society, 62-63.
Statutory law, 4.
Substantive law, 27.
Suits,
  of corporations of religious institutes, 97.
  possessory, 57-58.
  proprietary, 57-58.
Suits, between,
  autonomous monasteries, 96.
  different clerical institutes, 96.
  different monasteries, 96.
  provinces, 96.
  same lay religious community, 96.
  same non-exempt religious institute, 96.
Summons, the, 110.
Superior, procedural rights of, 33.
Superioress, procedural rights of, 33.
Suspension of moral person, 40, 115-117.
Syndic, appointment of, 43.
  office of, 41, 44.
  ratification of, 43.
Syndicus, defined, 21-23.

Theory of moral person, fiction, 2.
  realist, 2.
Tort, action of, 40, 59, 114.
Trial,
  consent of corporate body for, 34-36, 102-105.
  contentious, defined, 55.
  corporate representation in, 23-24, 29, 61.
  criminal, defined, 55-56.
  object of, 56.
  subject matter of, 60.
Tribunal, religious,
  jurisdiction of, 95.

Universitas personarum, 18.
Universitas bonorum, 18.

Withdrawal of rights, by penalty, 114.

CANON LAW STUDIES*

1. Freriks, Rev. Celestine A., C.PP.S., J.C.D., Religious Congregations in Their External Relations, 121 pp., 1916.
2. Galliher, Rev. Daniel M., O.P., J.C.D., Canonical Elections, 117 pp., 1917.
3. Borkowski, Rev. Aurelius L., O.F.M., J.C.D., De Confraternitatibus Ecclesiasticis, 136 pp., 1918.
4. Castillo, Rev. Cayo, J.C.D., Disertacion Historico-Canonica sobre la Potestad del Cabildo en Sede Vacante o Impedida del Vicario Capitular, 99 pp., 1919 (1918).
5. Kubelbeck, Rev. William J., S.T.B., J.C.D., The Sacred Penitentiaria and Its Relation to Faculties of Ordinaries and Priests, 129 pp., 1918.
6. Petrovits, Rev. Joseph J. C., S.T.D., J.C.D., The New Church Law on Matrimony, X-461 pp., 1919.
7. Hickey, Rev. John J., S.T.B., J.C.D., Irregularities and Simple Impediments in the New Code of Canon Law, 100 pp., 1920.
8. Klekotka, Rev. Peter J., S.T.B., J.C.D., Diocesan Consultors, 179 pp., 1920.
9. Wanenmacher, Rev. Francis, J.C.D., The Evidence in Ecclesiastical Procedure Affecting the Marriage Bond, 1920 (Printed 1935).
10. Golden, Rev. Henry Francis, J.C.D., Parochial Benefices in the New Code, IV-119 pp., 1921 (Printed 1925).
11. Koudelka, Rev. Charles J., J.C.D., Pastors, Their Rights and Duties According to the New Code of Canon Law, 211 pp., 1921.
12. Melo, Rev. Antonius, O.F.M., J.C.D., De Exemptione Regularium, X-188 pp., 1921.
13. Schaaf, Rev. Valentine Theodore, O.F.M., S.T.B., J.C.D., The Cloister, X-180 pp., 1921.
14. Burke, Rev. Thomas Joseph, S.T.D., J.C.D., Competence in Ecclesiastical Tribunals, IV-117 pp., 1922.
15. Leech, Rev. George Leo, J.C.D., A Comparative Study of the Constitution "Apostolicae Sedis" and the "Codex Juris Canonici," 179 pp., 1922.
16. Motry, Rev. Hubert Louis, S.T.D., J.C.D., Diocesan Faculties According to the Code of Canon Law, II-167 pp., 1922.
17. Murphy, Rev. George Lawrence, J.C.D., Delinquencies and Penalties in the Administration and the Reception of the Sacraments, IV-121 pp., 1923.

* Below n. 100 only the following numbers are still available: Nn. 3, 4, 9, 25, 34, 57 and 75. Beginning with n. 100 only the following are unavailable: Nn. 100-111 inclusive, and n. 113.

18. O'Reilly, Rev. John Anthony, S.T.B., J.C.D., Ecclesiastical Sepulture in the New Code of Canon Law, 11-129 pp., 1923.
19. Michalicka, Rev. Wenceslas Cyril, O.S.B., J.C.D., Judicial Procedure in Dismissal of Clerical Exempt Religious, 107 pp., 1923.
20. Dargin, Rev. Edward Vincent, S.T.B., J.C.D., Reserved Cases According to the Code of Canon Law, IV-103 pp., 1924.
21. Godfrey, Rev. John A., S.T.B., J.C.D., The Right of Patronage According to the Code of Canon Law, 153 pp., 1924.
22. Hagedorn, Rev. Francis Edward, J.C.D., General Legislation on Indulgences, II-154 pp., 1924.
23. King, Rev. James Ignatius, J.C.D., The Administration of the Sacraments to Dying Non-Catholics, V-141 pp., 1924.
24. Winslow, Rev. Francis Joseph, O.F.M., J.C.D., Vicars and Prefects Apostolic, IV-149 pp., 1924.
25. Correa, Rev. Jose Servelion, S.T.L., J.C.D., La Potestad Legislativa de la Iglesia Catolica, IV-127 pp., 1925.
26. Dugan, Rev. Henry Francis, A.M., J.C.D., The Judiciary Department of the Diocesan Curia, 87 pp., 1925.
27. Keller, Rev. Charles Frederick, S.T.B., J.C.D., Mass Stipends, 167 pp., 1925.
28. Paschang, Rev. John Linus, J.C.D., The Sacramentals According to the Code of Canon Law, 129 pp., 1925.
29. Piontek, Rev. Cyrillus, O.F.M., S.T.B., J.C.D., De Indulto Exclaustrationis necnon Saecularizationis, XIII-289 pp., 1925.
30. Kearney, Rev. Richard Joseph, S.T.B., J.C.D., Sponsors at Baptism According to the Code of Canon Law, IV-127 pp., 1925.
31. Bartlett, Rev. Chester Joseph, A.M., LL.B., J.C.D., The Tenure of Parochial Property in the United States of America, V-108 pp., 1926.
32. Kilker, Rev. Adrian Jerome, J.C.D., Extreme Unction, V-425 pp., 1926.
33. McCormick, Rev. Robert Emmett, J.C.D., Confessors of Religious, VIII-266 pp., 1926.
34. Miller, Rev. Newton Thomas, J.C.D., Founded Masses According to the Code of Canon Law, VII-93 pp., 1926.
35. Roelker, Rev. Edward G., S.T.D., J.C.D., Principles of Privilege According to the Code of Canon Law, XI-166 pp., 1926.
36. Bakalarczyk, Rev. Richardus, M.I.C., J.U.D., De Novitiatu, VIII-208 pp., 1927.
37. Pizzuti, Rev. Lawrence, O.F.M., J.U.L., De Parochis Religiosis, 1927. (Not Printed.)
38. Bliley, Rev. Nicholas Martin, O.S.B., J.C.D., Altars According to the Code of Canon Law, XIX-132 pp., 1927.
39. Brown, Mr. Brendan Francis, A.B., LL.M., J.U.D., The Canonical Juristic Personality with Special Reference to its Status in the United States of America, V-212 pp., 1927.

40. Cavanaugh, Rev. William Thomas, C.P., J.U.D., The Reservation of the Blessed Sacrament, VIII-101 pp., 1927.
41. Doheny, Rev. William J., C.S.C., A.B., J.U.D., Church Property: Modes of Acquisition, X-118 pp., 1927.
42. Feldhaus, Rev. Aloysius H., C.PP.S., J.C.D., Oratories, IX-141 pp., 1927.
43. Kelly, Rev. James Patrick, A.B., J.C.D., The Jurisdiction of the Simple Confessor, X-208 pp., 1927.
44. Neuberger, Rev. Nicholas J., J.C.D., Canon 6 or the Relation of the Codex Juris Canonici to the Preceding Legislation, V-95 pp., 1927.
45. O'Keefe, Rev. Gerald Michael, J.C.D., Matrimonial Dispensations, Powers of Bishops, Priests, and Confessors, VIII-232 pp., 1927.
46. Quigley, Rev. Joseph A. M., A.B., J.C.D., Condemned Societies, 139 pp., 1927.
47. Zaplotnik, Rev. Johannes Leo, J.C.D., De Vicariis Foraneis, X-142 pp., 1927.
48. Duskie, Rev. John Aloysius, A.B., J.C.D., The Canonical Status of the Orientals in the United States, VIII-196 pp., 1928.
49. Hyland, Rev. Francis Edward, J.C.D., Excommunication, Its Nature, Historical Development and Effects, VIII-181 pp., 1928.
50. Reinmann, Rev. Gerald Joseph, O.M.C., J.C.D., The Third Order Secular of Saint Francis, 201 pp., 1928.
51. Schenk, Rev. Francis J., J.C.D., The Matrimonial Impediments of Mixed Religion and Disparity of Cult, XVI-318 pp., 1929.
52. Coady, Rev. John Joseph, S.T.D., J.U.D., A.M., The Appointment of Pastors, VIII-150 pp., 1929.
53. Kay, Rev. Thomas Henry, J.C.D., Competence in Matrimonial Procedure, VIII-164 pp., 1929.
54. Turner, Rev. Sidney Joseph, C.P., J.U.D., The Vow of Poverty, XLIX-217 pp., 1929.
55. Kearney, Rev. Raymond A., A.B., S.T.D., J.C.D., The Principles of Delegation, VII-149 pp., 1929.
56. Conran, Rev. Edward James, A.B., J.C.D., The Interdict, V-163 pp., 1930.
57. O'Neill, Rev. William H., J.C.D., Papal Rescripts of Favor, VII-218 pp., 1930.
58. Bastnagel, Rev. Clement Vincent, J.U.D., The Appointment of Parochial Adjutants and Assistants, XV-257 pp., 1930.
59. Ferry, Rev. William A., A.B., J.C.D., Stole Fees, V-136 pp., 1930.
60. Costello, Rev. John Michael, A.B., J.C.D., Domicile and Quasi-Domicile, VII-201 pp., 1930.
61. Kremer, Rev. Michael Nicholas, A.B., S.T.B., J.C.D., Church Support in the United States, VI-136 pp., 1930.
62. Angulo, Rev. Luis, C.M., J.C.D., Legislation de la Iglesia sobre la intencion en la application de la Santa Misa, VII-104 pp., 1931.

63. Frey, Rev. Wolfgang Norbert, O.S.B., A.B., J.C.D., The Act of Religious Profession, VIII-174 pp., 1931.
64. Roberts, Rev. James Brendan, A.B., J.C.D., The Banns of Marriage, XIV-140 pp., 1931.
65. Ryder, Rev. Raymond Aloysius, A.B., J.C.D., Simony, IX-151 pp., 1931.
66. Campagna, Rev. Angelo, Ph.D., J.U.D., Il Vicario Generale del Vescovo, VII-205 pp., 1931.
67. Cox, Rev. Joseph Godfrey, A.B., J.C.D., The Administration of Seminaries, VI-124 pp., 1931.
68. Gregory, Rev. Donald J., J.U.D., The Pauline Privilege, XV-165 pp., 1931.
69. Donohue, Rev. John F., J.C.D., The Impediment of Crime, VII-110 pp., 1931.
70. Dooley, Rev. Eugene A., O.M.I., J.C.D., Church Law on Sacred Relics, IX-143 pp., 1931.
71. Orth, Rev. Clement Raymond, O.M.C., J.C.D., The Approbation of Religious Institutes, 171 pp., 1931.
72. Pernicone, Rev. Joseph M., A.B., J.C.D., The Ecclesiastical Prohibition of Books, XII-267 pp., 1932.
73. Clinton, Rev. Connell, A.B., J.C.D., The Paschal Precept, IX-108 pp., 1932.
74. Donnelly, Rev. Francis B,. A.M., S.T.L., J.C.D., The Diocesan Synod, VIII-125 pp., 1932.
75. Torrente, Rev. Camilo, C.M.F., J.C.D., Las Procesiones Sagradas, V-145 pp., 1932.
76. Murphy, Rev. Edwin J., C.PP.S., J.C.D., Suspension Ex Informata Conscientia, XI-122 pp., 1932.
77. MacKenzie, Rev. Eric F., A.M., S.T.L., J.C.D., The Delict of Heresy in its Commission, Penalization, Absolution, VII-124 pp., 1932.
78. Lyons, Rev. Avitus E., S.T.B., J.C.D., The Collegiate Tribunal of First Instance, XI-147 pp., 1932.
79. Connolly, Rev. Thomas A., J.C.D., Appeals, XI-195 pp., 1932.
80. Sangmeister, Rev. Joseph V., A.B., J.C.D., Force and Fear as Precluding Matrimonial Consent, V-211 pp., 1932.
81. Jaeger, Rev. Leo A., A.B., J.C.D., The Administration of Vacant and Quasi-Vacant Episcopal Sees in the United States, IX-229 pp., 1932.
82. Rimlinger, Rev. Herbert T., J.C.D., Error Invalidating Matrimonial Consent, VII-79 pp., 1932.
83. Barrett, Rev. John D. M., S.S., J.C.D., A Comparative Study of the Third Plenary Council of Baltimore and the Code, IX-221 pp., 1932.
84. Carberry, Rev. John J., Ph.D., S.T.D., J.C.D., The Juridical Form of Marriage, X-177 pp., 1934.
85. Dolan, Rev. John L., A.B., J.C.D., The Defensor Vinculi, XII-157 pp., 1934.

86. HANNAN, REV. JEROME D., A.M., S.T.D., LL.B., J.C.D., The Canon Law of Wills, IX-517 pp., 1934.
87. LEMIEUX, REV. DELISE A., A.M., J.C.D., The Sentence in Ecclesiastical Procedure, IX-131 pp., 1934.
88. O'ROURKE, REV. JAMES J., A.B., J.C.D., Parish Registers, VII-109 pp., 1934.
89. TIMLIN, REV. BARTHOLOMEW, O.F.M., A.M., J.C.D., Conditional Matrimonial Consent, X-381 pp., 1934.
90. WAHL, REV. FRANCIS X., A.B., J.C.D., The Matrimonial Impediments of Consanguinity and Affinity, VI-125 pp., 1934.
91. WHITE, REV. ROBERT J., A.B., LL.B., S.T.B., J.C.D., Canonical Ante-Nuptial Promises and the Civil Law, VI-152 pp., 1934.
92. HERRERA, REV. ANTONIO PARRA, O.C.D., J.C.D., Legislacion Ecclesiastica sobra el Ayuno y la Abstinencia, XI-191 pp., 1935.
93. KENNEDY, REV. EDWIN J., J.C.D., The Special Matrimonial Process in Cases of Evident Nullity, X-165 pp., 1935.
94. MANNING, REV. JOHN J., A.B., J.C.D., Presumption of Law in Matrimonial Procedure, XI-111 pp., 1935.
95. MOEDER, REV. JOHN M., J.C.D., The Proper Bishop for Ordination and Dimissorial Letters, VII-135 pp., 1935.
96. O'MARA, REV. WILLIAM A., A.B., J.C.D., Canonical Causes for Matrimonial Dispensations, IX-155 pp., 1935.
97. REILLY, REV. PETER, J.C.D., Residence of Pastors, IX-81 pp., 1935.
98. SMITH, REV. MARINER T., O.P., S.T.Lr., J.C.D., The Penal Law for Religious, VII-169 pp., 1935.
99. WHALEN, REV. DONALD W., A.M., J.C.D., The Value of Testimonial Evidence in Matrimonial Procedure, XIII-297 pp., 1935.
100. CLEARY, REV. JOSEPH F., J.C.D., Canonical Limitations on the Alienation of Church Property, VIII-141 pp., 1936.
101. GLYNN, REV. JOHN C., J.C.D., The Promoter of Justice, XX-337 pp., 1936.
102. BRENNAN, REV. JAMES H., S.S., M.A., S.T.B., J.C.D., The Simple Convalidation of Marriage, VI-135 pp., 1937.
103. BBUNINI, REV. JOSEPH BERNARD, J.C.D., The Clerical Obligations of Canons 139 and 142, X-121 pp., 1937.
104. CONNOR, REV. MAURICE, A.B., J.C.D., The Administrative Removal of Pastors, VIII-159 pp., 1937.
105. GUILFOYLE, REV. MERLIN JOSEPH, J.C.D., Custom, XI-144 pp., 1937.
106. HUGHES, REV. JAMES AUSTIN, A.B., A.M., J.C.D., Witnesses in Criminal Trials of Clerics, IX-140 pp., 1937.
107. JANSEN, REV. RAYMOND J., A.B., S.T.L., J.C.D., Canonical Provisions for Catechetical Instruction, VII-153 pp., 1937.
108. KEALY, REV. JOHN JAMES, A.B., J.C.D., The Introductory Libellus in Church Court Procedure, XI-121 pp., 1937.
109. MCMANUS, REV. JAMES EDWARD, C.SS.R., J.C.D., The Administration of Temporal Goods in Religious Institutes, XVI-196 pp., 1937.

110. MORIARTY, REV. EUGENE JAMES, J.C.D., Oaths in Ecclesiastical Courts, X-115 pp., 1937.
111. RAINER, REV. ELIGIUS GEORGE, C.SS.R., J.C.D., Suspension of Clerics, XVII-249 pp., 1937.
112. REILLY, REV. THOMAS F., C.SS.R., J.C.D., Visitation of Religious, VI-195 pp., 1938.
113. MORIARITY, REV. FRANCIS E., C.SS.R., J.C.D., The Extraordinary Absolution from Censures, XV-334 pp., 1938.
114. CONNOLLY, REV. NICHOLAS P., J.C.D., The Canonical Erection of Parishes, X-132 pp., 1938.
115. DONOVAN, REV. JAMES JOSEPH, J.C.D., The Pastor's Obligation in Prenuptial Investigation, XII-322 pp., 1938.
116. HARRIGAN, REV. ROBERT J., M.A., S.T.B., J.C.D., The Radical Sanation of Invalid Marriages, VIII-208 pp., 1938.
117. BOFFA, REV. CONRAD HUMBERT, J.C.D., Canonical Provisions for Catholic Schools, VII-211 pp., 1939.
118. PARSONS, REV. ANSCAR JOHN, O.M.Cap., J.C.D., Canonical Elections, XII-236 pp., 1939.
119. REILLY, REV. EDWARD MICHAEL, A.B., J.C.D., The General Norms of Dispensation, XII-156 pp., 1939.
120. RYAN, REV. GERALD ALOYSIUS, A.B., J.C.D., Principles of Episcopal Jurisdiction, XII-172 pp., 1939.
121. BURTON, REV. FRANCIS JAMES, C.S.C., A.B., J.C.D., A Commentary on Canon 1125, X-222 pp., 1940.
122. MIASKIEWICZ, REV. FRANCIS SIGISMUND, J.C.D., Supplied Jurisdiction According to Canon 209, XII-340 pp., 1940.
123. RICE, REV. PATRICK WILLIAM, A.B., J.C.D., Proof of Death in Prenuptial Investigation, VIII-156 pp., 1940.
124. ANGLIN, REV. THOMAS FRANCIS, M.S., J.C.D., The Eucharistic Fast, VIII-183 pp., 1941.
125. COLEMAN, REV. JOHN JEROME, J.C.D., The Minister of Confirmation, VI-153 pp., 1941.
126. DOWNS, REV. JOSEPH EMMANUEL, A.B., J.C.D., The Concept of Clerical Immunity, XI-163 pp., 1941.
127. ESSWEIN, REV. ANTHONY ALBERT, J.C.D., Extrajudicial Penal Powers of Ecclesiastical Superiors, X-144 pp., 1941.
128. FARRELL, REV. BENJAMIN FRANCIS, M.A., S.T.L., J.C.D., The Rights and Duties of the Local Ordinary Regarding Congregations of Women Religious of Pontifical Approval, V-195 pp., 1941.
129. FEENEY, REV. THOMAS JOHN, A.B., S.T.L., J.C.D., Restitutio in Integrum, VI-169 pp., 1941.
130. FINDLAY, REV. STEPHEN WILLIAM, O.S.B., A.B., J.C.D., Canonical Norms Governing the Deposition and Degradation of Clerics, XVII-279 pp., 1941.
131. GOODWINE, REV. JOHN, A.B., S.T.L., J.C.D., The Right of the Church to Acquire Property, VIII-119 pp., 1941.

132. Heston, Rev. Edward Louis, C.S.C., Ph.D., S.T.D., J.C.D., The Alienation of Church Property in the United States, XII-222 pp., 1941.
133. Hogan, Rev. James John, A.B., S.T.L., J.C.D., Judicial Advocates and Procurators, XIII-200 pp., 1941.
134. Kealy, Rev. Thomas M., A.B., Litt.D., J.C.D., Dowry of Women Religious, IX-152 pp., 1941.
135. Keene, Rev. Michael James, O.S.B., J.C.D., Religious Ordinaries and Canon 198, V-164 pp., 1942.
136. Kerin, Rev. Charles A., S.S., M.A., S.T.B., J.C.D., The Privation of Christian Burial, XVI-279 pp., 1941.
137. Louis, Rev. William Francis, M.A., J.C.D., Diocesan Archives, X-101 pp., 1941.
138. McDevitt, Rev. Gilbert Joseph, A.B., J.C.D., Legitimacy and Legitimation, X-247 pp., 1941.
139. McDonough, Rev. Thomas Joseph, A.B., J.C.D., Apostolic Administrators, X-217 pp., 1941.
140. Meier, Rev. Carl Anthony, A.B., J.C.D., Penal Administration Procedure Against Negligent Pastors, XI-240 pp., 1941.
141. Schmidt, Rev. John Rogg, A.B., J.C.D., The Principles of Authentic Interpretation in Canon 17 of the Code of Canon Law, XII-331 pp., 1941.
142. Slafkosky, Rev. Andrew Leonard, A.B., J.C.D., The Canonical Episcopal Visitation of the Diocese, X-197 pp., 1941.
143. Swoboda, Rev. Innocent Robert, O.F.M., J.C.D., Ignorance in Relation to the Imputability of Delicts, IX-271 pp., 1941.
144. Dubé, Rev. Arthur Joseph, A.B., J.C.D., The General Principles for the Reckoning of Time in Canon Law, VIII-299 pp., 1941.
145. McBride, Rev. James T., A.B., J.C.D., Incardination and Excardination of Seculars, XX-585 pp., 1941.
146. Krol, Rev. John T., J.C.D., The Defendant in Ecclesiastical Trials, XII-207 pp., 1942.
147. Comyns, Rev. Joseph J., C.SS.R., A.B., J.C.D., Papal and Episcopal Administration of Church Property, XIV-155 pp., 1942.
148. Barry, Rev. Garrett Francis, O.M.I., J.C.D., Violation of the Cloister, XII-260 pp., 1942.
149. Bolduc, Rev. Gatien, C.S.V., A.B., S.T.L., J.C.D., Les Études dans les Religions Cléricales, VIII-155 pp., 1942.
150. Boyle, Rev. David John, M.A., J.C.D., The Juridic Effects of Moral Certitude on Pre-Nuptial Guarantees, XII-188 pp., 1942.
151. Canavan, Rev. Walter Joseph, M.A., Litt.D., J.C.D., The Profession of Faith, XII-143 pp., 1942.
152. Desrochers, Rev. Bruno, A.B., Ph.L., S.T.B., J.C.D., Le Premier Concile Plénier de Québec et le Code de Droit Canonique, XIV-186 pp., 1942.

153. Dillon, Rev. Robert Edward, A.B., J.C.D., Common Law Marriage, X-148 pp., 1942.
154. Dodwell, Rev. Edward John, Ph.D., S.T.B., J.C.D., The Time and Place for the Celebration of Marriage, X-156 pp., 1942.
155. Donnellan, Rev. Thomas Andrew, A.B., J.C.D., The Obligation of the Misa pro Populo, VII-131 pp., 1942.
156. Eltz, Rev. Louis Anthony, A.B., J.C.L., Cooperation in Crime.
157. Gass, Rev. Sylvester Francis, M.A., J.C.D., Ecclesiastical Pensions, XI-206 pp., 1942.
158. Guiniven, Rev. John Joseph, C.SS.R., J.C.D., The Precept of Hearing Mass, XIV-188 pp., 1942.
159. Gulczynski, Rev. John Theophilus, J.C.D., The Desecration and Violation of Churches, X-126 pp., 1942.
160. Hammill, Rev. John Leo, M.A., J.C.D., The Obligations of the Traveler According to Canon 14, VIII-204 pp., 1942.
161. Haydt, Rev. John Joseph, A.B., J.C.D., Reserved Benefices, XI-148 pp., 1942.
162. Huser, Rev. Roger John, O.F.M., A.B., J.C.D., The Crime of Abortion in Canon Law, XII-187 pp., 1942.
163. Kearney, Rev. Francis Patrick, A.B., S.T.L., J.C.L., The Principles of Canon 1127
164. Linahen, Rev. Leo James, S.T.L., J.C.D., De Absolutione Complicis In Peccato Turpi, 114 pp., 1942.
165. McCloskey, Rev. Joseph Aloysius, A.B., J.C.D., The Subject of Ecclesiastical Law According to Canon 12, XVII-246 pp., 1942.
166. O'Neill, Rev. Francis Joseph, C.SS.R., J.C.D., The Dismissal of Religious in Temporary Vows, XIII-220 pp., 1942.
167. Prince, Rev. John Edward, A.B., S.T.D., J.C.D., The Diocesan Chancellor, X-136 pp., 1942.
168. Riesner, Rev. Albert Joseph, C.SS.R., J.C.D., Apostates and Fugitives from Religious Institutes, IX-168 pp., 1942.
169. Stenger, Rev. Joseph Bernard, J.C.D., The Mortgaging of Church Property, 186 pp., 1942.
170. Waldron, Rev. Joseph Francis, A.B., J.C.D., The Minister of Baptism, XII-197 pp., 1942.
171. Willett, Rev. Robert Albert, J.C.D., The Probative Value of Documents in Ecclesiastical Trials, X-124 pp., 1942.
172. Woeber, Rev. Edward Martin, M.A., J.C.D., The Interpellations, XII-161 pp., 1942.
173. Benko, Rev. Matthew Aloysius, O.S.B., M.A., J.C.L., The Abbot *Nullius*.
174. Christ, Rev. Joseph James, M.A., S.T.L., J.C.L., Dispensation from Vindicative Penalties.
175. Clancy, Rev. Patrick M. J., O.P., A.B., S.T.Lr., J.C.D., The Local Religious Superior, X-299 pp., 1943.

176. Clarke, Rev. Thomas James, J.C.D., Parish Societies, XII-147 pp., 1943.
177. Connolly, Rev. John Patrick, S.T.L., J.C.D., Synodal Examiners and Parish Priest Consultors, X-223 pp., 1943.
178. Drumm, Rev. William Martin, A.B., J.C.L., Hospital Chaplains.
179. Flanagan, Rev. Bernard Joseph, A.B., S.T.L., J.C.D., The Canonical Erection of Religious Houses, X-147 pp., 1943.
180. Kelleher, Rev. Stephen Joseph, A.B., S.T.B., J.C.D., Discussions with non-Catholics: Canonical Legislation, X-93 pp., 1943.
181. Lewis, Rev. Gordian, C.P., J.C.D., Chapters in Religious Institutes, XII-169 pp., 1943.
182. Marx, Rev. Adolph, J.C.D., The Declaration of Nullity of Marriages Contracted Outside the Church, X-151 pp., 1943.
183. Matulenas, Rev. Raymond Anthony, O.S.B., A.B., J.C.L., Communication, a Source of Privileges.
184. O'Leary, Rev. Charles Gerard, C.SS.R., J.C.D., Religious Dismissed After Perpetual Profession, X-213 pp., 1943.
185. Power, Rev. Cornelius Michael, J.C.L., The Blessing of Cemeteries.
186. Shuhler, Rev. Ralph Vincent, O.S.A., J.C.D., Privileges of Regulars to Absolve and Dispense, XII-195 pp., 1943.
187. Ziolkowski, Rev. Thaddeus Stanislaus, A.B., J.C.D., The Consecration and Blessing of Churches, XII-151 pp., 1943.
188. Heneghan, Rev. John Joseph, S.T.D., J.C.L., The Marriages of Unworthy Catholics: Canons 1065 and 1066.
189. Carroll, Rev. Coleman Francis, M.A., S.T.L., J.C.L., Charitable Institutions.
190. Ciesluk, Rev. Joseph Edward, Ph.B., S.T.L., J.C.L., National Parishes in the United States.
191. Coburn, Rev. Vincent Paul, A.B., J.C.L., Marriages of Conscience.
192. Connors, Rev. Charles Paul, C.S.Sp., A.B., J.C.L., Extra-Judicial Procurators in the Code of Canon Law.
193. Coyle, Rev. Paul Raymond, A.B., J.C.L., Judicial Exceptions.
194. Fair, Rev. Bartholomew Francis, A.B., S.T.L., J.C.L., The Impediment of Abduction.
195. Gallagher, Rev. Thomas Raphael, O.P., A.B., S.T.Lr., J.C.L., The Examination of the Qualities of the Ordinand.
196. Gannon, Rev. John Mark, S.T.L., J.C.L., The Interstices Required for the Promotion to Orders.
197. Goldsmith, Rev. J. William, B.C.S., S.T.L., J.C.L., The Competence of Church and State over Marriage—Disputed Points.
198. Goodwine, Rev. Joseph Gerard, A.B., S.T.B., J.C.L., The Reception of Converts.
199. Kowalski, Rev. Romuald Eugene, O.F.M., A.B., J.C.L., Sustenance of Religious Houses of Regulars.
200. McCoy, Rev. Alan Edward, O.F.M., J.C.L., Force and Fear in Relation to Delictual Imputability and Penal Responsibility.

201. McDevitt, Rev. Vincent John, Ph.B., S.T.L., J.C.L., Perjury.
202. Martin, Rev. Thomas Owen, Ph.D., S.T.D., J.C.L., Adverse Possession, Prescription and Limitation of Actions: The Canonical "Praescriptio."
203. Miklosovic, Rev. Paul John, A.B., J.C.L., Attempted Marriages and Their Consequent Juridic Effects.
204. Mundy, Rev. Thomas Maurice, A.B., S.T.L., J.C.L., The Union of Parishes.
205. O'Dea, Rev. John Coyle, A.B., J.C.L., The Matrimonial Impediment of Nonage.
206. Olalia, Rev. Alexander Ayson, S.T.L., J.C.L., A Comparative Study of the Christian Constitution of States and the Constitution of the Philippine Commonwealth.
207. Poisson, Rev. Pierre-Marie, C.S.C., A.B., Ph.L., Th.L., J.C.L., Droits Patrimoniaux des Maisons et des Eglises Religieuses.
208. Stadalnikas, Rev. Casimir Joseph, M.I.C., J.C.L., Reservation of Censures.
209. Sullivan, Rev. Eugene Henry, S.T.L., J.C.L., Proof of the Reception of the Sacraments.
210. Vaughan, Rev. William Edward, J.C.L., Constitutions for Diocesan Courts.
211. Paro, Rev. Gino, S.T.D., J.C.L., The Right of Apostolic Legation.
212. Balzer, Rev. Ralph Francis, C.P., J.C.L., The Computation of Time in a Canonical Novitiate.
213. Dougherty, Rev. John Whelan, A.B., S.T.L., J.C.L., De Inquisitione Speciali.
214. Dziob, Rev. Michael Walter, J.C.L., The Sacred Congregation for the Oriental Church.
215. Eidenschink, Rev. John Albert, O.S.B., B.A., J.C.L., The Election of Bishops in the Letters of Pope Gregory the Great.
216. Gill, Rev. Nicholas, C.P., J.C.L., The Spiritual Prefect in Clerical Religious Houses of Study.
217. Hynes, Rev. Harry Gerard, S.T.L., J.C.D., The Privileges of Cardinals, XII-183 pp., 1945.
218. McDevitt, Rev. Gerald Vincent, S.T.L., J.C.D., The Renunciation of an Ecclesiastical Office, XIV—179 pp., 1946.
219. Manning, Rev. Joseph Leroy, J.C.L., The Free Conferral of Offices.
220. Meyer, Rev. Louis G., O.S.B., A.B., S.T.B., J.C.D., Alms-Gathering by Religious, XII—163 pp., 1946.
221. O'Donnell, Rev. Cletus Francis, M.A., J.C.L., The Marriage of Minors.
222. Prunskis, Rev. Joseph, J.C.D., Comparative Law, Ecclesiastical and Civil, in Lithuanian Concordat, X—161 pp., 1945.
223. Sweeney, Rev. Francis Patrick, C.SS.R., J.C.D., The Reduction of Clerics to the Lay State, X—199 pp., 1945.

224. Vogelpohl, Rev. Henry John, J.C.L., The Simple Impediments to Holy Orders.
225. Brockhaus, Rev. Thomas Aquinas, O.S.B., A.B., J.C.L., Religious who Are Known as *Conversi.*
226. Griese, Rev. Orville Nicholas, S.T.D., J.C.L., Marriage and the Procreation of Offspring.
227. Boudreaux, Rev. Warren Louis, J.C.L., The *"ab acatholicis nati"* of Canon 1099, § 2.
228. Bowe, Rev. Thomas Joseph, A.B., J.C.L., Religious Superioresses.
229. Diederichs, Rev. Michael Ferdinand, S.C.J., J.C.L., The Jurisdiction of the Latin Ordinaries over their Oriental Subjects.
230. Dingman, Rev. Maurice John, A.B., S.T.L., J.C.L., The Plaintiff in Contentious Trials.
231. Frison, Rev. Basil, C.M.F., M.Mus., J.C.L., The Retroactivity of Law.
232. Galvin, Rev. William Anthony, M.A., J.C.L., The Administrative Transfer of Pastors.
233. Goracy, Rev. Joseph C., J.C.L., The Diriment Impediment of Major Orders.
234. Hale, Rev. Joseph Francis, M.A., S.T.L., J.C.L., The Pastor of Burial.
235. Henry, Rev. Joseph Arthur, A.B., J.C.L., The Mass and Holy Communion: Inter-Ritual Law.
236. Linenberger, Rev. Herbert, C.PP.S., J.C.L., The False Denunciation of an Innocent Confessor.
237. Lowry, Rev. James Martin, A.B., J.C.L., Dispensation from Private Vows.
238. Lynch, Rev. George Edward, A.B., S.T.L., J.C.L., Coadjutors and Auxiliaries of Bishops.
239. Lynch, Rev. Timothy, M.S.SS.T., J.C.L., Contracts between Bishops and Religious Congregations.
240. McClunn, Rev. Justin David, A.B., S.T.L., J.C.L., Administrative Recourse.
241. Lohmuller, Rev. Martin M., The Promulgation of Law.
242. McGrath, Rev. James, A.B., J.C.L., The Privilege of the Canon.
243. Marbach, Rev. Joseph Francis, A.B., J.C.L., Marriage Legislation for the Catholics of the Oriental Rites in the United States and Canada.
244. Shimkus, Rev. Bernard Aloysius, A.B., J.C.L., The Determination and Transfer of Rite.
245. Smith, Rev. Vincent Michael, A.B., S.T.L., J.C.L., Ignorance Affecting Matrimonial Consent.
246. Wachtrle, Rev. Paul Anthony, A.B., J.C.L., The Baptism of the Children of Non-Catholics.

247. Crotty, Rev. Matthew M., J.C.L., The Recipient of First Holy Communion.
248. Eagleton, Rev. George, J.C.L., The Quinquennial Faculties, Formula IV.
249. Gibbons, Rev. Marion L., C.M., LL.B., J.C.L., Domicile of The Wife Unlawfully Separated from Her Husband.
250. Kelly, Rev. Bernard M., S.T.L., J.C.L., The Functions Reserved to Pastors.
251. Kilcullen, Rev. Thomas J., LL.M., J.C.L., The Collegiate Moral Person as Party Litigant.
252. Lafontaine, Rev. Germain J., W.F., J.C.L., Relations Canoniques entre Le Missionnaire et Ses Superieurs.
253. Lane, Rev. Loras T., A.B., S.T.L., J.C.L., Matrimonial Procedure in the Ordinary Court of Second Instance.
254. Lover, Rev. James F., C.SS.R., J.C.L., The Master of Novices.
255. McNicholas, Rev. Timothy J., J.C.L., The *Septimae Manus* Witness.
256. Marositz, Rev. Joseph J., M.S.C., J.C.L., Obligations and Privileges of Religious Promoted to the Episcopal or Cardinalitial Dignities.
257. Murphy, Rev. Francis J., A.B., J.C.L., Legislative Powers of the Provincial Council.
258. O'Brien, Rev. Romaeus W., O.Carm., J.C.L., The Provincial Superior in Religious Orders of Men.
259. Pfaller, Rev. Benedict A., O.S.B., J.C.L., The *Ipso Facto* Effected Dismissal oi Religious.
260. Popek, Rev. Alphonse S., M.A., J.C.L., The Rights and Obligations of Metropolitans.
261. Ristuccia, Rev. Bernard J., C.M., J.C.L., Quasi-Religious.
262. Sonntag, Rev. Nathaniel L., O.F.M.Cap., J.C.L., Censorship of Special Classes of Books.
263. Stadler, Rev. Joseph N., J.C.L., Frequent Holy Communion.
264. Szal, Rev. Ignatius J., J.C.L., The Communication of Catholics with Schismatics.
265. Wagner, Rev. Urban S., O.F.M. Conv., J.C.L., Parochial Substitute Vicars and Supplying Priests.

www.ingramcontent.com/pod-product-compliance
Lightning Source LLC
LaVergne TN
LVHW050221080826
844660LV00012B/447

* 9 7 8 0 8 1 3 2 2 4 2 9 9 *